AFTER T]

G000096127

To Alison, Zoë, Olivia and James

Also by Ian Grant

PLAYS
Stella Europa
Thomas Boleyn

NON-FICTION
The City at War
The Countryside at War

After the Ball

BY IAN GRANT

Julia —

*Thank you so very much
for your wonderful creation
of Blanche in all her complexity
and tribulation — and the
warmth and love that you gave
to her.*

With very best wishes.

Ian

Cornwall Editions

First published 2018
by Cornwall Editions Ltd
52 Gladsmuir Road,
London N19 3JU

ISBN 978-1-904880-35-6

This version of the text went to print before the end of rehearsals
and may differ slightly from the version performed.

All professional enquiries regarding this play
should be addressed to:

Creative Structure Ltd,
52 Gladsmuir Road,
Upper Holloway,
London N19 3JU, UK

www.creativestructure.net
ian.grant@creativestructure.net

+44 776 418 7452

Printed and bound by Lightning Source UK

Cover photo by Nick Rutter, design by Rebecca Pitt

The first performance of *After the Ball* was given on 7th March 2018 at Upstairs at the Gatehouse, London.

Cast, in alphabetical order

Jack Bennett	Albert Kerridge
Mark Carlisle	Ted Turner / M. Lépine / Bar guest
Stuart Fox	William Randall
Elizabeth Healey	Margery / Marguerite / Nurse
Emily Tucker	Joyce Randall / Bar guest
Julia Watson	Blanche Randall

Creative crew

Director	**Nadia Papachronopoulou**
Assistant Director	Hannah Sands
Production manager	Callum Finn
Stage manager	Grace Lewis
Set and costume design	Natalie Pryce
Lighting design	George Bach
Composition and sound design	Chris Drohan
Publishing design	Steven Maddocks
Social media marketing	Amy Liette Hunter
Photography	Mitzi de Margary
General manager	Ashley Cook
Executive Producers	Niall Bishop, Ian Grant

After the Ball was produced by

TIME Productions

Author's Note

Through the stories of the characters in *After the Ball* I have tried to express some of my core beliefs – we are what we do; what we do can never be undone; our acts have ripple (or explosive) effects long after the act itself; women and men are entirely equal; individual and state violence to other human beings is unforgiveable.

In *After the Ball* we follow a south London family from 1914 to 1971. A similar tale could be told about any European city family who suffered and persevered through the catastrophic wars of the 20th century. It's a story of resilience in the face of personal trauma. It's a story of political and social bonds that get stretched beyond breaking point. It's story of female liberation and political emancipation and the triumphs and challenges these bring. *After the Ball* came to the stage in the centenary anniversary year of the end of the First World War; on the centenary of the first votes for women in British political history; and opened on International Women's Day, March 8th 2018.

The play emphasises the role of the individual within a social and political context – we see women and men campaigning for the right to vote, for equality in society and for their ability to choose a way of life. We see women and men falling in love, making good and bad decisions, working as best they can to survive in a society pummelled twice in thirty years by world war. Within that framework is the key theme – that we are all individually responsible for our own actions.

The script tells the story of the characters through naturalistic scenes within a formal, poetic framework. The play moves backwards and forwards in time from 1914 to 1971. The arc of the story is emotional, not chronological. The set is an open abstract space within which the actors create their stories through the immediacy of their voices and bodies in space and time. The stage vision reflects the brightness of young hopes and the fierce bruising of experience.

I try to write rich new leading roles for older actors, and particularly older female actors. The lack of new material of some of our greatest actors is both a flaw and a huge opportunity in theatre and film today. In my work I stick to the principle that we have at least equal numbers of women and men in the cast. In *After the Ball,* the actors have to be highly flexible and shift their sense of older and younger selves sometimes in instant transitions across time from scene to scene. I hope actors will find the roles meaty and satisfying.

I'm delighted to have to have worked with Nadia Papachronopoulou as the director of the play. Nadia is a young Greek director who had already worked extensively in British theatre, and she brought to this British story her woman's insight and her European sensibility. In her reading of the script she found things I didn't know were there, under the surface. She was the conductor to my composer, and enriched the script through rehearsal with her high energy and artistic skill.

Ian Grant
Upper Holloway, London, February 2018

Director's Note

I am a director with a passion for new writing that aims to broaden our cultural understanding of theatre, as I believe art can provoke a shift in ideas and culture. Ian Grant's *After the Ball* provides us with a unique perspective of what happens after war, from the people that went and the people who were left behind.

As a director, I find that establishing a creative relationship with a writer is an incredibly inspiring process, as together you create entire worlds, tackle issues, and build characters that engage and entertain an audience. I am particularly interested in directing new writing, as I am in being a part of something fresh that hasn't been done before, which intellectually and emotionally challenges me to examine rigorously my own practice as an artist. I believe the director is an interpretive artist who unpicks the words on the page and examines the relationships created on paper. Theatre is all about working collaboratively and taking the written word and making it live and breathe in a theatrical space.

What struck me most when I first read *After the Ball* was the interplay between the characters and how the family ties evolve through the play. For me, the play's challenge and beauty lie in the fact it spans sixty years, so the actors, the audience and myself really get to explore the core of the characters' development through the course of their lives, ranging from their twenties to their sixties. Our leading characters William and Blanche Randall are played by the fantastic Stuart Fox and Julia Watson, who I have worked with previously at the Orange Tree Theatre, Richmond when I was the theatre's Resident Trainee Director five years ago. I am delighted to get to work with them again on this play, which is quite demanding both physically and emotionally as all the characters go on such a big journey.

I am fascinated by the representation of women in the play, specifically in the mother-daughter relationships and how complicated and delicate they are. It is very interesting to see the different generations of women in the play and how they shift and change through time, as the play starts in 1914 when women in Britain did not have the vote and goes to the 1970s when women had gained greater independence. The female characters (and the effect the shifting social and political dynamics of the twentieth century had on them) are of paramount importance to this play.

The play explores the theme of memory, which is one that has a great deal of scope for design, imaginative staging, and the breadth for audience members to be transported from their seats into the world of the play. Natalie Pryce, our designer, transformed the space at Upstairs at the Gatehouse, and I was really eager to see how our audience responded to this urgent and thought-provoking piece.

Nadia Papachronopoulou
London, February 2018

SETTING
Inner south London, the Belgian countryside near Ypres and the
English south coast.

The action moves forward and back in time, between 1914 and 1973.

CAST
Three women, three men.

CHARACTERS

Blanche Randall	Seamstress, William's wife / Bar guest. Age in the play 29–83.
Joyce Randall	Secretary, daughter of Blanche and William/Bar guest. Age in the play 18–49.
William Randall	Telephone engineer and soldier. Blanche's husband. Age in the play 28–84.
Margery	Junior foreign office official / Nurse / Marguerite Lépine. Age in the play 23–55.
Albert Kerridge	Motor mechanic and soldier. Age in the play 27–80.
Ted Turner	Army sergeant / M. Lépine / Bar guest. Age in the play 31–59.

Their dates of birth:
M. Lépine – 1868; Ted – 1884; Blanche – 1885; William – 1886;
Albert – 1887; Margery/Marguerite – 1891; Joyce – 1919.

NOTE ON THE TEXT
A blank line following a character's name indicates a silence or pause.
A forward stroke towards the end of a line, followed by another word
or two, indicates that the next character's words are spoken over the
words after the stroke.

Introit

Silence, summer light
MARGUERITE, aged 27, comes. She is picking the petals from a flower.
She sings:

MARGUERITE: Après la guerre finie,[1]
Les soldats anglais partient.
Les mademoiselles toujours beaucoup pleuraient
Après la guerre finie.

MARGUERITE goes

Music fades in: 'After the Ball is Over'[2]

Scene One

May 1914, London, – a small public bar
WILLIAM (28), ALBERT (27), MARGERY (23)
Bar guests are on stage, singing 'After the Ball is Over'.

ALBERT: Why don't you marry Blanche? She needs a husband.

WILLIAM: Does she?

ALBERT: They all do, one way or another.

WILLIAM: She was very quiet.

ALBERT: They can be deep, though, women.

WILLIAM: Know a lot?

ALBERT: I'm a married man now.

WILLIAM: Is Vera deep, Albert?

ALBERT: No, she's lovely.

WILLIAM: From your wide knowledge of women, is Blanche deep?

ALBERT: I don't know. But you could do worse than find out.

WILLIAM: There's no time for being married. You haven't noticed, but there's a war coming. We've got to stop it. I've got to go, I'm speaking tonight.

ALBERT: Will, you're 28. If you're going to get on, you need a good woman.

WILLIAM: Women support me. Proper international socialists. They hate war.

ALBERT: What do you come home to, Will? No-one to talk to. Dark room, no fire burning. Let me tell you, as a married man –

WILLIAM: It's the older men that's the problem, they want to be in with the / government –

ALBERT: – as a married man, my Vera is my pride and joy. Warm house in the winter, lamps lit, steak and onions on the table. I tell her what's going on. And a cuddle, Will. A good old cuddle. Nothing like it, winter or summer. You mark my words.

WILLIAM: There's no time for all that. We're splitting, the British Socialist Party is breaking up. We've got to stand by our comrades in Europe.

ALBERT: I'd rather lie down by my Vera. When did you last have a girl, Will? I wouldn't look at another one, now, not since I married Vera. She gets lovelier by the day, filling out in all the right places. Opening up. Like a flower.

WILLIAM: Why Blanche?

ALBERT: She's still good-looking, very shapely. She's waiting for it Will.

WILLIAM:

ALBERT: Look, her father got killed in the Boer War, there's not much to live on. She's a very nice young woman, handy with her needle, turns herself out nice and tidy. Comes from a good family.

WILLIAM: Your family?

ALBERT: Think about it. If you can find a moment in your busy
            life.

WILLIAM: You should come to the meeting.

ALBERT: British Socialists? Half of them want to stop a war, the
            other lot think war would be a jolly good thing, sort
            out a government they don't like.

WILLIAM: You've not got hold of it, Albert. We're a force. All over
            Europe, it's the same as here. We're rising, the working
            classes are on the march. The strikes are breaking the
            back of the bosses and if they don't give over, there's
            going to be big trouble.

MARGERY comes

ALBERT: I think trouble's arrived. Hallo dear. You're looking
            particularly lovely tonight.

WILLIAM: I tell you, there's going to be trouble.

MARGERY: Now then, Albert Kerridge, none of your nonsense.
            You're a married man.

ALBERT: I think I'm entitled to offer a lady a touch of old-
            fashioned hospitality. Move over, Will, let the lady sit
            down.

WILLIAM: No, I must be off. Excuse me.

ALBERT: No, no, no. That's not polite, Will. Margery, this is
            William Randall.

MARGERY: Yes, how do you do, Mr Randall?

WILLIAM: How do you do, Miss –?

MARGERY: Oh, call me Margery, please. Very well indeed, thank
            you very much.

ALBERT: Will you join us in a drink?

MARGERY: Well, that's very kind, I don't mind if I do. What are you
            having?

WILLIAM: I'm sorry I don't mean to be rude, I'm speaking at the
            War Memorial Hall tonight.

ALBERT: Will's teetotal, he doesn't count. What about a small
            glass of port?

MARGERY: Just the ticket.

ALBERT moves upstage to order her a drink

MARGERY: You're teetotal, then?

WILLIAM: That's right.

MARGERY: Just don't fancy it?

WILLIAM: Something like that.

MARGERY: Warms you up though. I don't overdo it, mind. But
            every now and again. You must have taken a drop once
            or twice.

WILLIAM: No. My father –

MARGERY: You're speaking?

WILLIAM: Yes.

MARGERY: Votes for women?

WILLIAM: No. Not tonight. British Socialist Party. It's a crisis.

MARGERY: Oh dear.

WILLIAM: We're the working class against the war but men are
             wavering – they think country is more important than
             class, pulling up drawbridges, supporting the war
             parties.

MARGERY: I hope we're not going to / war –

WILLIAM: We've built a mass movement, we've disrupted the
             imperialists, we're demanding a true compact between /
             capital and labour.

MARGERY: I don't like all the / strikes –

WILLIAM: – but they're falling for the imperialists' propaganda,
             they're going over to the other side. I must go.

ALBERT returns

ALBERT: Here you are, Margery. Down the hatch!

MARGERY: Bottoms up!

ALBERT: You know my cousin, Blanche.

MARGERY: Very nice girl.

ALBERT: Just right for Will. Tell you what, Margery, you have a
             word with Vera, see if I'm right, see if she doesn't say
             the same.

WILLIAM: Now, half a mo.

MARGERY: I expect you know Blanche.

WILLIAM: No. We met once or twice.

MARGERY: She's a lovely soul. Very clever with her needlework.
             Looks after her mother so well.

ALBERT: Let's have a day out.

WILLIAM: I've got things on.

ALBERT: Margery, you ask Vera.

MARGERY: We'll go out. The weather's lovely, I'll find a friend, you
             and Vera, Blanche and Will, we'll all go out for a day in
             the country.

Noise of bar-room babble rises and fades

Scene Two

July 1914, a London street, evening
WILLIAM (28), BLANCHE (29)

BLANCHE: Thank you for walking me home, William.

WILLIAM: You're welcome, Blanche. I hope you enjoyed the meeting.

BLANCHE: You needn't take me to my door. I can look after myself.

WILLIAM: I will, if I may, Blanche.

BLANCHE:
            Yes, you may. Miss Billinghurst[3] is an unusual woman.

WILLIAM: Stuck in that invalid chair but she's so strong.

BLANCHE: I don't agree with her.

WILLIAM: She's like a soldier, firing off her crutches like rifles.

BLANCHE: Yes, she's military. I don't like that.

WILLIAM: She's fighting hard for the cause.

BLANCHE: The Women's Social and Political Union doesn't need warlike women.

WILLIAM: We're right behind them in the BSP.

BLANCHE: Warlike women?

WILLIAM: No, no. Votes for women.

BLANCHE: Are you sure? Your right-wing people are edging
           towards war, aren't they?

WILLIAM: You know a lot.

BLANCHE: I live quietly, with Mother. When I'm not working, I
           read.

WILLIAM:

BLANCHE:

WILLIAM: What do you read?

BLANCHE: The newspapers. I read them to Mother.

WILLIAM: I hope she's well.

BLANCHE: She stays indoors.

WILLIAM: Your father / fought –

BLANCHE: He died in South Africa.

WILLIAM: I'm sorry he didn't come back.

BLANCHE: We were out picking blackberries. Mother, Father and
           me. I carried the basket. He said I have to go away, just
           for a bit. I thought he would be back soon.

WILLIAM: My father was in that campaign / as well –

BLANCHE: You spoke well at the meeting. It's quite brave to stand
           up in front of all those people.

WILLIAM: Women should have the vote. We're all equal. For ever,
           women have been cut out of power. We study it at
           the BSP. Miss Billinghurst's a good speaker. It makes

no sense for women not to have the vote. Women are equal to men in every way and should have the right to decide.

BLANCHE: About what?

WILLIAM: War and peace. We try to work out what's happening. We've got groups all over the country. And in Europe. Big socialist parties in France and Germany. Speakers come over. Some fellows from our group went to Germany.

BLANCHE: To Germany?

WILLIAM: Oh yes. Many people there think the war talk is madness. It makes no sense, the workers know it. We have so much in common with our comrades over there. But German industry is building a huge war machine.

BLANCHE: Another war would be horrible.

WILLIAM: Germany is rising, they've been chasing us for years. They want an empire, like ours. Our fathers were defending it.

BLANCHE: Mother took it very hard. She doesn't talk about it.

WILLIAM: Life can be so different – that's what we say. If we work together we can give everyone a chance. Same with women and votes. We say share the power, share the work, share a better life. The way it is, Germany should settle for what she already has. But their ruling class wants an empire, like us and France.

BLANCHE: And can't they have one?

WILLIAM: Where would they find one, now? I'm glad you came to the meeting.

BLANCHE: Yes.

WILLIAM: Did you enjoy the day out with Vera and Albert and the others?

BLANCHE: Yes, it was very nice.

WILLIAM: I enjoyed it too.

WILLIAM: What do you want to do?

BLANCHE: Pardon?

WILLIAM: I mean – in life.

BLANCHE: I live with Mother. I sew. I work for the draper. I do the work at home. I have a machine.

WILLIAM: Albert said you're very good at it. I'm at the County of London Electricity Supply Company. We do a lot of work for the Post Office.

BLANCHE: Albert said.

WILLIAM: There's a big future in the telephones. The Post Office is buying up the small exchanges – big new equipment coming in. Got my certificates on the new gear, lot of work coming in. Do you have brothers?

BLANCHE: No.

WILLIAM: Very quiet at home.

BLANCHE:

WILLIAM: Except when Albert turns up.

BLANCHE: We don't see Albert often. Mother doesn't encourage
            visitors.

WILLIAM: I don't live at home now. Set up on my own.

BLANCHE: The day out was very nice.

WILLIAM: You know Margery, then.

BLANCHE: She's very independent. She teases Albert. I don't know
            her very well, or her friend. Do you know him?

WILLIAM: No. Very lucky with the weather.

BLANCHE: I liked the place we ate, down by the river. The air was
            very fresh.

WILLIAM: Did you like it? Albert said he thought you would.

BLANCHE: Mother's frightened about war. I try to calm her. You
            were strong in the debate tonight.

WILLIAM: I wondered, Blanche –

BLANCHE: Yes?

WILLIAM: I wondered – would you like to come to another of our
            meetings?

BLANCHE: I'll speak to Mother.

WILLIAM: Blanche, let me walk you to your door.

BLANCHE and WILLIAM go

Scene Three

1937, the Randalls' kitchen (the living room – sink, cooker etc are offstage, in the scullery)
JOYCE (18), WILLIAM (51), BLANCHE (52)
WILLIAM is at the table.

JOYCE comes

JOYCE: Dad, I've got it. The letter's come. They want me to start next week.

WILLIAM: My little girl, going out to work, all grown-up.

JOYCE: I've to be there at nine o'clock and meet Dr White, he's the one I'm going to be working for, I met him for a few minutes at the interview, I hope I'll manage, I don't know how fast he dictates. What am I going to wear?

WILLIAM: You'll look grand, whatever you wear.

JOYCE: It's in Bedford Square, the trees will look lovely in the summer. I'll sit there and eat my sandwich at midday with the other girls. There are shops just round the corner so if there's time I can get anything I need.

WILLIAM: It'll sort itself / out –

JOYCE: They actually start at half past eight so I must be out of the door by twenty-five to, so up at six. But I won't mind. Same as you. They chose me Dad, I've got myself a job.

BLANCHE comes, with shopping bags

JOYCE: Mum, they want me.

BLANCHE: That's good dear. Take this bag for me, would you.

JOYCE: Here's the letter.

BLANCHE: Just pop it on the table.

JOYCE: I'm going to be working for the Deputy Director, taking notes, going out to meetings, using my shorthand.

WILLIAM: He was impressed by your exam results, I'll be bound.

JOYCE: I had to do a test there and then, before they interviewed me. What do you think I should wear, Mum?

BLANCHE: I'm very pleased for you, dear. You're a clever girl.

JOYCE: Not a girl, Mum. I'm going out to work.

BLANCHE: What about that nice green dress we made you last year?

JOYCE: Thirty-five shillings a week. I'm going to pay my way. Help with the shopping.

WILLIAM: You don't need to do that. You've got your train fares, money for dinner, bits and pieces you'll have to spend. You and Mum go and look for something new to wear on your first day.

BLANCHE: She doesn't need to be extravagant. The green dress is hardwearing, she'll get good use from it.

WILLIAM: She'll need more than one, something new / to start her off.

BLANCHE: She's going out to work, not the dance hall. We'll go and look at material, choose a pattern. I'll make

you another one dear and we'll look through your
cupboard, you've got plenty to wear.

JOYCE: I'm going to town. Every day. New people to meet. All
those people. And I'm going to be one of them with a
job to do. Earning my money. Busy. Busy, busy, busy.
And the theatres.

BLANCHE: Come and help me with these bags.

WILLIAM: Let her be, Blanche. It's very good news. I'll bring the
bags into the scullery.

BLANCHE: I can manage.

JOYCE: It's all right, Mum. I'm hungry. I'll help you with the
vegetables.

Scene Four

June 1915, the Randalls' kitchen
WILLIAM (29), BLANCHE (30), ALBERT (28), MARGERY (24)
BLANCHE and MARGERY at the table

MARGERY: Lovely wedding. But they're all over in a flash. You didn't dance much.

BLANCHE: I never learned.

MARGERY: You can take it up.

BLANCHE: I'm very busy with the sewing. The war's made a difference. People want more done.

MARGERY: Take an evening off.

BLANCHE: I should be here when Will comes home. I hate this war. I don't know what all these women think who shout at men who haven't volunteered, calling them all sorts of names. I would never do that to William.

MARGERY: Vera thinks Albert's going to join up. She says he should do his duty.

BLANCHE: It's his duty to look after Vera, make a home for them.

MARGERY: Do you want a family, Blanche?

BLANCHE: I hate it. Six months ago it was all flags and marching bands. 'All over by Christmas'. Just lies. They told us lies.

MARGERY: Do you want a baby?

BLANCHE: Now we're fighting all over France and Belgium,
            we're fighting in Greece, we're fighting in Persia, we're
            fighting in Africa. William was right. He said it was an
            imperial war, just like the last one.

MARGERY: Do you want to give William a baby?

BLANCHE:

MARGERY: Do you?

BLANCHE: I don't know how. Mother never said.

MARGERY: Blanche, dear, your mother's not dead. She saw you
            being married. She told you what to do.

BLANCHE: No. She didn't.

MARGERY: What happened on your wedding night? Did Will - did
            he - did he - come to you? In bed?

BLANCHE: I think so.

MARGERY: We'll either he did or he didn't. You must know.

BLANCHE: I didn't know what to expect.

MARGERY: Has he done the same thing since?

BLANCHE: Yes.

MARGERY: Often?

BLANCHE: Yes. Well, sometimes. More at first.

MARGERY: Do you like what he does?

BLANCHE: I didn't. I'm getting used to it.

MARGERY: Do you like it now?

BLANCHE: I don't know what he wants, Margery. I sometimes feel he likes me and sometimes I don't know where he is. I don't know whether he thinks I'm a good wife.

MARGERY: Of course you're a good wife and he should be jolly grateful he has you. Men are like children – they strut around like cockerels making a hullabaloo, and haven't a sensible idea in their heads, half the time.

BLANCHE: You're kind.

MARGERY: No I'm not, but I know men better than you. And I can hear them coming in the door, so I'll be off.

BLANCHE: No stay a while, please.

WILLIAM and ALBERT come

BLANCHE: I'll put the kettle on.

BLANCHE goes

WILLIAM: Just what we need, Blanche. Albert, sit down, sit.

ALBERT: Vera thinks I should join up. There's a bit of a push on at work, chap came round, chivvying everybody up. Turner, you know him – Ted Turner. Although you have to call him Sergeant now.

BLANCHE: *(offstage)* Albert, you're not going to go over there and get yourself killed. Why would Vera say that?

ALBERT: There's many women do.

MARGERY: Many women don't have enough to do.

ALBERT: I passed a crowd this morning, waving their hats and
             their feathers.

WILLIAM: Those fellows we had over last year were right -
             Germany going to push out.

BLANCHE comes with tea.

BLANCHE: You said they were reasonable men.

WILLIAM: They were. They're in our line of work. It's
             the bosses and the landed classes driving this on.

ALBERT: But it's the lads causing all the problems in Belgium.
             Dirty work, killing the women and children.

WILLIAM: That's all in the papers.

ALBERT: Look at today's *Daily Mirror*. Gas. They're pumping gas
             over the countryside.

BLANCHE: That's awful.[4]

ALBERT: It says here – 'By using asphyxiating gas fumes the
             Germans north of Ypres have forced back French
             troops to the Yser Canal'[5].

WILLIAM: Clouds of gas?

ALBERT: First a bombardment, then this new thing, pumping
             huge clouds of gas over the countryside. Killed half a
             division of the French army in half an hour. The rest
             ran away.

BLANCHE: Men surely can't do that. Decent men wouldn't do that.

WILLIAM: You get swept up in things. You follow orders and find
             yourself doing things.

BLANCHE: You won't get swept up in this. You don't believe in it.

WILLIAM: There are rights and wrongs.

BLANCHE: You want to stop the war.

WILLIAM: You can hear the guns from here, up the top of the hill.

BLANCHE: I hate that sound, William.

ALBERT: That's why we have to stop it.

BLANCHE: Albert, don't try to persuade him.

MARGERY: I'm off. Coming on the bus, Albert?

ALBERT: I told Vera I'd be straight back.

MARGERY: Well, now you're in trouble. Come along.

ALBERT: Think about it, Will. Thank you for the tea, Blanche.

MARGERY and ALBERT go

BLANCHE: William, you're not going to join up? I don't want
            you to go and be killed.

WILLIAM: I said it, didn't I, when the party split. All over Europe
            the socialist parties lost their nerve and voted for war.
            It's torn us apart. The bosses are driving it, last year
            they persuaded the politicians to beat up the storm
            about Austria punishing Serbia for killing the Arch-
            Duke, Russia defending Serbia, the Kaiser lashing out.
            And who's in the trenches? Us. Who gets drowned
            when the ships are sunk? Us. We're fighting our
            comrades.

BLANCHE: The Germans aren't us. They're the ones killing the Belgians.

WILLIAM: Yes they are, Blanche. Don't you see? We have an empire. The French have an empire. The Tsar has an empire. The German bosses want an empire to supply their raw materials. That's why they've invaded Belgium, to get at all the coal.

BLANCHE: We haven't invaded Belgium.

WILLIAM: No, of course we haven't.

BLANCHE: So why are the Germans us?

WILLIAM: The German workers are us. They're our comrades. They want the same as we do.

BLANCHE: You mean an empire.

WILLIAM: No, Blanche, not an empire. Fair distribution.

BLANCHE: You said the Germans wanted an empire.

WILLIAM: The bosses. The German bosses.

BLANCHE: But we have an empire. It's no surprise the Germans want one. It's been happening for years.

WILLIAM: That's not the point. Our empire is a fact of history. It's our job to make it socialist. Before the war the Socialist International brought us all together. Slowly, inevitably, there's progress. Like votes for women – they started the international movement in Germany ten years ago.

BLANCHE: But it hasn't happened. The Socialists went the other way, voted for war. Now you think this new Union of Democratic Control will do some good.

WILLIAM: It's going to be strong – good men in it. And women.
            Equal citizenship between men and women. This war
            is a lie. The Germans are swindling their own people.
            Our government's just as bad.

BLANCHE: It's horrible what they're doing.

WILLIAM: They can't do it by force, just invade other countries.
            Rule has to be democratic. That's why women must
            have the vote and the political and economic power
            distributed, shared right across all the people.

BLANCHE: Would you like us to have a family?

WILLIAM:

BLANCHE: We could do what you like. I'm getting used to it. In
            our bed.

WILLIAM: Now? A child?

BLANCHE: We'd be a family. Like other families.

WILLIAM: It hasn't happened yet. We haven't – made one.

BLANCHE: I don't know how. Mother didn't say. Vera will help me.
            And Margery. And we'll do it together. I'd like to. Sit
            down.

WILLIAM: Killing people with clouds of gas. It's not on.

BLANCHE: How, William? It's become so big, so fast. Something
            wicked spreading over the world.

WILLIAM: I must go and change.

BLANCHE: You haven't drunk your tea.

WILLIAM: I have to go out to a meeting. I'm speaking.

BLANCHE: Not tonight, William. This gas frightens me. The
             airships might come back. I want us to be a family.
             We're married.

WILLIAM: Albert may be right.

BLANCHE: No, you're right. All your letters to the people in France
             and Germany and Italy – all of them, that's the future,
             standing together. You tell me that and it's true. You
             have to go on believing that, you and all the men like
             you who do the work, you stand together.

WILLIAM: Some of our best people have changed their minds.

BLANCHE: I'm standing with you. Men killing men like this is not
             right.

WILLIAM: The poison is in the wind, Blanche.

BLANCHE: Stay with me. Stay strong. Don't go out tonight.

Scene Five

July 1915. Army recruiting office.
WILLIAM (29), ALBERT (28), TED (31)
TED sits at the table. A folding screen, open, is on stage

TED: Next.

WILLIAM comes

TED: Name?

WILLIAM: William Randall.

TED: British subject?

WILLIAM: Yes.

TED: Date of birth?

WILLIAM: May 5th 1886.

TED: Trade or calling?

WILLIAM: Electrician.

TED: Ever been in His Majesty's forces?

WILLIAM: No.

TED: Fit?

WILLIAM: Yes.

TED: Yes, what?

WILLIAM: Yes, I'm fit.

TED: Yes, I'm fit what?

WILLIAM:

TED: Do you want to join the army?

WILLIAM: Yes.

TED: Yes, Sergeant. If you want to join the army, then it's 'yes
            Sergeant' when you address me or 'sir' for any soldier
            of higher rank.

WILLIAM: I'm not in the army yet.

TED: Listen, Mister Randall. Thousands of men better than
            you have joined up for King and Country. The King
            has asked us to do a job for him. General Kitchener has
            asked us to do a job for him. Our wives and families
            have asked us to do a job for them. Are you married?

WILLIAM: Yes. Sergeant.

TED: What does Mrs Randall say about you volunteering?

WILLIAM: She doesn't know.

TED: Qualifications?

WILLIAM: Matriculation. Electrician, first class. Telephone power
            supply.

TED: Tell me about your work on the telephones.

WILLIAM: I worked on the central exchange, wiring it up, big new
            equipment.

TED: Like that sort of work?

WILLIAM: It's good work. Gets people talking to each other.

TED: What do they say? *(He calls)* Nurse.

NURSE comes

TED: This one's William Randall. Go behind that screen and take off your shirt and trousers.

WILLIAM: No doctor?

TED: We've run out of doctors.

NURSE and WILLIAM move behind screen

TED: Next.

ALBERT comes

TED: Name?

ALBERT: Albert Kerridge.

TED: British subject?

ALBERT: Yes.

TED: Date of birth?

ALBERT: August 12th 1887.

NURSE: *(from behind screen)* Breathe in.

TED: Trade or calling?

ALBERT: Motor vehicles. You behind there, Will?

TED: Never you mind about him. What to do with motor
            vehicles?

NURSE: Open your mouth. Say aaah.

ALBERT: Suspension, mostly. Flat springs, new coil springs,
            mainly steel, some new alloy, but they're not so good.

TED: Alright, alright, I don't need a bloody lecture about
            springs.

NURSE: Sergeant! *(To WILLIAM)* Stand up straight please.

TED: Excuse my French, Nurse. Ever been in His Majesty's
            forces?

ALBERT: No, Sergeant.

TED: Fit?

NURSE: Cough.

WILLIAM coughs

ALBERT: Whoa, what's she holding on to Will?

TED: Mr Kerridge, I said are you fit?

ALBERT: If she's as lovely as they say, I'm fit for it, Sergeant.

TED: Enough of your lip, Mr Kerridge, if you were in the
            Army, by now you'd be on parade on your own in full
            dress. Are you married?

ALBERT: To the lovely Mrs Vera Kerridge, Sergeant.

TED: She know you're here?

ALBERT: Yes, Sarge. She said I should do my duty.

NURSE: Do up your trousers, Mr Randall.

ALBERT: Have you done your duty, Will?

TED: Qualifications?

ALBERT: Matriculation. Mechanic, second class. City and Guilds
            mathematics.

TED: Nurse. Albert Kerridge. Go behind that screen and take
            off your shirt and trousers.

ALBERT: Stand by your beds, Nurse.

WILLIAM: *(emerging from behind screen)* If it's going to be like this,
            Albert, you'd better let Vera know before you sign up.

TED: It's not going to be like this, Randall. It's hard, it's nasty,
            your mates get killed in the mud. You're going to be
            marching all over France and Belgium and God knows
            where else with Kaiser Bill trying to shoot you, gas you
            or blow you to bits.

NURSE: *(from behind the screen)* Breathe in.

WILLIAM: But we've pushed them back, Sergeant.

TED: That's what they say. But Jerry's a hard nut. He'll be back.

WILLIAM: I follow it in the papers. We have to stop them.

TED: I know all about that. It's not a picnic in the park,
            Randall. But you have the right spirit. What's Mrs
            Randall going to say?

WILLIAM: She's anti-militarist. I try to explain it to her.

NURSE: *(from behind the screen)* Say Aaaah.

ALBERT: Aaaah. I bet I can make you say it too.

TED: Well, now's your chance to make her proud of you.
            There's bloodshed and murder of brave men, helpless
            women and little children over there in Belgium. It's
            only by sending out more men that we can be sure
            of keeping similar bloodshed and murder out of
            England[6]. Any family in the Army?

WILLIAM: Father was, Sergeant.

TED: Which regiment?

WILLIAM: Queen's Own Royal West Kent.

NURSE: Stand up straight.

NURSE squeals

WILLIAM: He reached Sergeant.

TED: Retired?

NURSE: Cough.

ALBERT coughs loud and long. NURSE squeals again

TED: Nurse. Have you got the blue form for Randall?

NURSE appears from behind the screen, slightly mussed.

TED: Thank you Nurse. All in order?

NURSE smooths her skirt and returns behind the screen.

WILLIAM: Retired as a private.

TED reviews the blue form cursorily

TED: Did he drink?

WILLIAM: Not any more. He went teetotal.

TED: Then you'd better watch your step. Does he know?

WILLIAM: Dead, Sergeant.

TED: Put your hand on this Testament and read out the oath.

WILLIAM: I, William Randall, swear by Almighty God, that I will
             be faithful and bear thus allegiance to His Majesty King
             George the Fifth, His Heirs and Successors, and that I
             will, as in duty bound, honestly and faithfully defend
             His Majesty, His Heirs and Successors, in Person,
             Crown and Dignity against all enemies.

TED: Good lad. Your pay is 1s. 3d a day, starting today. Take
             this shilling. The rest'll be made up. Go home and tell
             Mrs Randall. There's no running away in the army.
             Forget your father. I dare say he wasn't much use to
             your mother. But you could make up for that. You'll
             know other lads, all pulling together in the King's
             service.

NURSE: Pull up your trousers, Mr Kerridge.

TED: Once we clear out the Boche our womenfolk, including
             Mrs Randall, will be safer, our children will grow up
             safe – and you'll have done your bit. Here's where you
             sign.

WILLIAM signs

             You'll get a letter telling you where to report. Make sure
             you're there. You're in the army now. Next.

Scene Six

August 1915; the Randalls' kitchen
BLANCHE (30), WILLIAM (29)

BLANCHE: Why didn't you tell me?

WILLIAM: I've got to, Blanche. Everyone's got to do their bit.
Albert's going. We all thought about it, talked it over
at the Company and at the meeting the other evening.
Miss Billinghurst was speaking –

BLANCHE: Oh her. You think what she says is more important
than me. But we don't agree with them. They know too
many people in the government. They all know each
other. They think they know us but they don't.

WILLIAM: It's happened. We're fighting. We can only stop it now
by fighting harder, pushing them back.

BLANCHE: It took my father. It drove your father to drink.

WILLIAM: Just a few months.

BLANCHE: It's taking you. That's what they said last year. You
didn't believe it then.

WILLIAM: We can't let it go on. Ted Turner came down to the
Company / and he said –

BLANCHE: Where are you, William? The man I married. The man
who told us the working class were standing up to the
imperialist bosses. The man who faced the fire of Miss
Billinghurst's crutches. You're leaving me alone.

WILLIAM: Vera's letting Albert go.

BLANCHE: You think it's all grand with the uniforms and the bands and Albert and the others all off to war, all boys together. You said you loved me, you married me, I looked up to you because you believe in things, we believe the same things and you work hard, we're making the house nice, one day it might be our own. And you go and join up behind my back, without saying anything, without even asking what I think.

WILLIAM: What you think?

BLANCHE: Yes, William, what I think. I sew, I cook, I clean the house, I do the washing – and I think. I thought a lot when I lived at home with Mother because she didn't say anything. I think a lot when you are out arguing, making speeches, sorting out the world. And I'm proud of you William, do you know that? But I deserve some consideration when you decide to join up and go to war.

WILLIAM: You should have come to the meeting. You would have understood.

BLANCHE: I don't need to go to Miss Billinghurst's meetings. You're married to me, not her. You should have talked to me. You don't care what I feel. You want to get away from me.

WILLIAM: No, Blanche, no, you're my wife, this is our home. When I'm back we'll start a family / and -

BLANCHE: You'll be killed. I love you, William, I won't let you go. Your job's important, we're doing good work we believe in. I need you to keep us whole.

WILLIAM: There's only one way to stop it.

BLANCHE: You can't stop it. Take back the shilling and tell them
you've changed your mind.

WILLIAM: I can't do that.

BLANCHE: You don't want to do it.

WILLIAM: It's too late.

BLANCHE: I see. I thought you loved me.

WILLIAM: It's too late. I'm in the army. I've orders to go.

Scene Seven

August 1939, the Randalls' kitchen
WILLIAM (53), BLANCHE (54), JOYCE (20)
WILLIAM is at the table, tuning a radio. BLANCHE is sewing.

JOYCE comes

JOYCE: I can't stop, Mum, I'm late.

BLANCHE: Where are you going, dear?

JOYCE: Old Vic. Kay's getting there early.

BLANCHE: Kay. She'll get herself into trouble one of these days, with that man of hers.

JOYCE: No, she won't, Mum. She's very careful.

BLANCHE: Well, I'm worried about her and so's her mother. You mind out, dear, and make sure you catch the train home.

JOYCE: I've arranged to stay with Kay tonight.

BLANCHE: You didn't tell us.

WILLIAM: Listen. They're saying the Germans and the Russians have made a pact. Russia should be with us.

JOYCE: I don't think they are Dad.

WILLIAM: We get on with the Russians. We're in touch with them, they came over.

BLANCHE: How many of you are going to the play?

WILLIAM: Good men, they were.

BLANCHE: Is Kay going with that man?

JOYCE: I don't know all Russia works like that.

BLANCHE: Is she going with that man?

JOYCE: Yes, Mum, she is.

BLANCHE: Are you going with someone?

WILLIAM: They've been going at it for twenty years. Our people could do the same.

JOYCE: Not everyone wants to be the same.

BLANCHE: Who're you going with, dear?

JOYCE: Just a friend of Kay's.

WILLIAM: But they're running the show. The workers are organising, taking the decisions.

JOYCE: It's different, Dad. Our way's democracy and elections.

BLANCHE: I don't want you staying out with a stranger.

WILLIAM: Our way's too slow. It keeps the bosses on top and the workers having to fight.

JOYCE: He's a friend of Kay's.

BLANCHE: Her choice isn't much to go by.

WILLIAM: They had a go, all at once. We had a go, in the Strike. We kept everything going.

JOYCE: We're going dancing, after the play.

WILLIAM: We organised and could have kept it going.

BLANCHE: I don't think you should be staying out with Kay and two men so late.

WILLIAM: Come on, Blanche, Joyce wants to enjoy herself.

JOYCE: I'll be all right, Mum.

BLANCHE: That Kay is going to get herself into trouble. I don't want Joyce going the same way.

JOYCE: Oh, Mum. I must dash, I'll miss the train.

WILLIAM: Let her go and have a dance.

WILLIAM re-tunes the radio

WILLIAM: We met at a dance.

BLANCHE: It's not good for her. That man Kay's got hanging around's not up to much. If it's a friend of his Joyce's going with, then I don't like it.

JOYCE: Mum, I'm off.

JOYCE goes

BLANCHE: We didn't dance.

WILLIAM: You were shy. Quiet.

BLANCHE: I might have danced.

WILLIAM: You didn't dance.

BLANCHE: How do you know?

WILLIAM: You were sitting down.

BLANCHE: You didn't ask me.

WILLIAM: I didn't know you, the first time.

BLANCHE: What about when you did know me? What about at our wedding?

WILLIAM: I don't remember, Blanche. It was a long time ago.

BLANCHE: You danced with that Margery.

WILLIAM: I asked you, but you were getting all the sandwiches and cake and such like.

BLANCHE: I didn't know what was happening.

WILLIAM: Your mother was there.

BLANCHE: She didn't tell me anything.

WILLIAM: You forget.

BLANCHE: I don't forget. There was nothing to forget. She didn't say anything to me.

WILLIAM: What should she have said?

BLANCHE: She should have told me what to do. You didn't tell me anything either.

WILLIAM: Long time ago now.

BLANCHE: I was waiting for you. Waiting to be married. Waiting to sit with you and be at home and be your wife. Then you went off.

WILLIAM: I went to the war.

BLANCHE: We were married.

WILLIAM: Lots of married men signed up.

BLANCHE: They came back, back to their homes.

WILLIAM: I came back, Blanche. I came home when the job was done.

BLANCHE: I had to drag you back.

WILLIAM: I came back, Blanche, to carry on with our lives, after the war. Bring up Joyce.

BLANCHE: Yes, that's right. For Joyce.

WILLIAM starts to whistle softly, turns up the radio. BLANCHE goes. Radio becomes quiet.

Explosion

Scene Eight

November 1917. Battlefield near Ypres, Belgium
ALBERT (30), TED (33), WILLIAM (31), MARGUERITE (26)
WILLIAM is prone at the edge of the stage. Neither TED nor ALBERT
see WILLIAM.

Explosion.

ALBERT comes, crawling, TED grips his arm. ALBERT yells in pain.

ALBERT: I'm smashed.

TED feels his arms. ALBERT cries out.

TED: Your drinking arm. Can you wiggle your fingers? You'll
            live. This hole's wet. It stinks.

ALBERT: We came through a horse. It's lying behind us.

TED: A bloody horse's guts.

ALBERT: I don't know which end it was. Couldn't see no head.
            Smell its belly.

TED: We're stuck here till Jerry's had his fill.

Explosion

TED: Oh bloody hell. Did Will catch it?

ALBERT: I don't know. He was on top of the wall. Almighty
            bang, knocked me down. I didn't see him. The tanks
            had mucked up all the bloody wires. Signals were out.
            I don't know where he is. We never had this problem
            before the tanks. It's bloody stupid, charging the
            bleeding tanks all over the lines. Horses and mules

were all right. The Rolls vehicles aren't so bad. It's the suspension, keeps them bouncing a bit so they don't grind down like the tracks. Good springs, new coil springs, mainly steel, some new alloy, but / they're not so good –

TED: All right, shut up. He can't be far away.

ALBERT: God knows where he is.

TED: Well, we need to get him.

Explosion

ALBERT: My arm's smashed.

TED: You wait here. I'll come back.

ALBERT: With this bloody stinking horse?

TED: Well, we need him. He knows his stuff. Which way do I go?

ALBERT: He'd just gone past a smashed-up brick shed. He wanted to get some of the lines up out of the mud.

TED: Alright. I'll find it. You wait here.

Sound of faint gunfire.

ALBERT: I'm coming with you, Sergeant.

TED: Good lad. We've only lost two from this platoon since we came out and I don't propose to lose any more.

ALBERT gets up, cries in pain as he leans on his arm. Explosion and flash

TED: Bloody hell.

ALBERT and TED go

Noise of gunfire fades. Light becomes ethereal. MARGUERITE comes. She approaches WILLIAM, gazes at him, kneels and cradles his head.

MARGUERITE: Papa! Papa! Il est blessé. Viens, Papa, aide-moi!

Light fades as MARGUERITE continues to hold WILLIAM

Scene Nine

December 1917, the Randalls' bedroom
WILLIAM (31), BLANCHE (32)
WILLIAM is lying on the bed. BLANCHE is dressing WILLIAMs
wounded legs.

BLANCHE: It's not weeping as much as it was. I'm going to put a bit
of iodine on it. It'll sting again.

She wipes a cloth over the wounds. WILLIAM grits his teeth and
breathes in sharply. She stops and continues a few times.

WILLIAM: You're not bad at this, Blanche.

BLANCHE: That's all right then.

WILLIAM: Better than some of them in the field hospital.

BLANCHE begins to wrap a bandage around each of WILLIAM's
thighs

BLANCHE: I don't know how they manage, with all those guns
going off.

WILLIAM: No guns there. Rows of men shot to pieces, moaning
and groaning, crying out, all day and all night. It stinks,
Blanche. Butcher's shop, all the meat going bad. You're
lying there, piece of meat. They had to get the shrapnel
out of my leg with a carving knife.

BLANCHE: You said.

WILLIAM: Bloke next to me told me to shut up, he'd had his leg off
so what was I complaining about. The nurse had to put
her fingers in me to get the piece out.

BLANCHE: You told me.

WILLIAM: I'm lucky. You'll never see it. Lines of them. On and on.
Smashed up men.

BLANCHE: They lost their son, up the road.

WILLIAM: The bloke the other side was dead in the morning. Just
gone. They covered him up, wheeled him off.

BLANCHE: She was crying her eyes out.

WILLIAM: Their boys were just like us. I came across them.
After their last big push we stopped them, they
couldn't go on. We began to move them back, finding
their trenches. Some of them got left behind as they
retreated. I was working my way across, laying new
wires and I heard them. I was on my own, I thought,
'Oh lord, now what?' I couldn't go back. I picked up my
rifle and released the catch. I could hear them, quietly
talking. If they'd heard me or seen me, that would've
been it. I was so cold. I thought there's only one way
to go. I stood up and walked towards the trench. As
I got to the edge and looked over, I shouted at them
and pointed my rifle. They were like tired rabbits, they
hadn't heard me coming. They scarcely moved, their
eyes were sunk. I don't know who was more frightened,
them or me.
      I pointed my rifle and waved them up. There was
about five or six of them. They didn't seem to have any
kit, they were just left behind. I shouted, 'Come on'.
They just stood there. 'Kommen', I said.
      And then they started to come up out of the
trench, very slowly. I was so cold I was shivering but
they didn't seem to be making any fuss or trying to do
anything. And they came up and looked at me. I didn't
know what to do so I waved my rifle and pointed back
to our lines. One by one they turned. 'That's right', I
shouted, 'Keep going'. I thought they would turn round

and come for me at any moment. But they just trudged on. It took ages, but they were done for, dazed, and just walked on. I saw our lines and shouted, 'Prisoners, prisoners'. Heads came up from our trench, went down and came up with cocked rifles as my little party walked towards them.

Then we were there, my Germans were taken in, my knees went and I just went down and the boys were cheering and making a noise. One of them picked up my rifle. He said 'how many shots did you have to fire?' I said I hadn't pulled the trigger. He said 'The magazine's empty'.

BLANCHE: You didn't want to shoot. I'm so proud of you. Lie down. I'm not going to lose you. Bend your legs up. How you didn't break your bones, I don't know. Poor Albert's in a worse state than you are.

WILLIAM: I wouldn't be here without him. He came out again, him and the Sergeant, to get me. If he hadn't done that he would be alright.

BLANCHE: That was brave of him.

WILLIAM: The Sergeant was the one. He didn't want to lose me.

BLANCHE: Albert didn't either, I'm sure.

WILLIAM: The Sergeant, Ted, he was the one. Blanche, I've got to go back soon.

BLANCHE: But you're finished with it.

WILLIAM: Job's not done.

BLANCHE: Finished with it. I'm going to look after you. They'll see that.

WILLIAM: The Sergeant said I have special skills.

BLANCHE: We were only just married. I've kept this house warm for us.

WILLIAM: We've broken them. But they're strong, could come back at us.

BLANCHE: You've done your job.

WILLIAM: Back out of the mud, over the river. Drier ground. Break through. Dry ground.

BLANCHE: We can be together again. I couldn't sleep.

WILLIAM: I'm in the army. I was called up.

BLANCHE: No you weren't. You volunteered. I won't have it. You've been away almost two years. I haven't seen you, I haven't hardly heard from you. You're wounded. I want you here. I'm your wife. You were very brave.

She touches him lightly

BLANCHE: Let me finish your bandages.

WILLIAM: I have to go.

BLANCHE: But why you, William? You can't do this on your own. Stay with me.

WILLIAM: We have to push them back, so there's a clean sheet.

BLANCHE: I joined the local committee of the East London Federation. There was a big majority in the Commons for women to get the vote, but there's more to do, now we can work together again. This is our work.

WILLIAM: Raining, raining, raining. Coughing, aching, boots full of mud up to your knees caked in blood hungry cold tea. Hay.

BLANCHE: Where were you?

WILLIAM:

BLANCHE: Where?

WILLIAM: Billeted in a farmhouse. They killed his sons.

BLANCHE: Just you and the farmer?

WILLIAM: Just me and the farmer. And his daughter.

BLANCHE: How old is she?

WILLIAM: I don't know.

BLANCHE: Is she a child? Is she a woman?

WILLIAM: Mud and blood everywhere. Guns, our guns, their guns, tanks, walls crash down, great filthy trenches open up, men pile in.

WILLIAM grabs BLANCHE's hand

WILLIAM: Get down, Blanche. Lie down.

BLANCHE: Wait, I haven't finished. You'll hurt yourself.

WILLIAM: We're all right. Lie on your back.

BLANCHE: William. Stop, William. You don't know what you are doing. I'm not ready.

WILLIAM: Quiet, Blanche. Lie down.

BLANCHE: No, William. No, don't touch me. No.

WILLIAM: Lie down.

BLANCHE: No. No.

Interval

Scene Ten

1918 Belgium, the countryside in summer
WILLIAM (31), MARGUERITE (27), M. LEPINE (50)
WILLIAM and MARGUERITE come. WILLIAM is carrying a bunch
of daisies. As he walks, he limps a little.

WILLIAM: *(sings)* Bonjour ma chérie, comment allez vous?
                   Bonjour ma chérie, je promène avec vous.
                   Bonjour ma chérie, ça ne fait rien,
                   Voulez vous promenade avec moi ce soir?
                   Oui, oui, très bien.

MARGUERITE: Oh your silly songs, I do not understand.

WILLIAM: My French is bad.

MARGUERITE: No, you speak well.

WILLIAM: I wish I could speak your language. I feel like a child.

MARGUERITE: You are not a child. You are soldier.

WILLIAM: Soldiers are just boys.

MARGUERITE: Not like you.

WILLIAM: I like you. You make me forget everything.

MARGUERITE: I hope you do not forget me.

WILLIAM: Your father wants to chase me away.

MARGUERITE: I will not let him.

WILLIAM: He will chase me with his fork, over the fields, into the
             woods, across the stream, so that I run far, far away.

Away from you. Far away. So that you can marry your
cousin the butcher.

MARGUERITE: Oh, no. I will die. I will not be a butcher wife. He
will not chase you in the woods. I will throw my
body in front of him.

WILLIAM: I will stand in his way.

MARGUERITE: What do you say?

WILLIAM: So you throw your body in front of me.

MARGUERITE: You must not say this. I am not like this. I will not
walk with you if you say this.

WILLIAM: Oh I'm sorry. Margeurite, I'm sorry.

MARGUERITE: You think I am like other girls, they go with the
soldiers in our village. You soldiers come in our
houses, we don't know you. Some girls they don't
care, they take them in the wood or in hay in barn.
Soldier give them something, they make parties
and dances, they say they will always love. Next day
they go.

WILLIAM: I came back.

MARGUERITE: You are here now, but you will be the same.

WILLIAM: No, I have to stay. I have to help. All the power to the
towns, the factories, the juice to the houses, it has to be
put back.

MARGUERITE: How long?

WILLIAM: When it's over, it'll be better. Germany will play by the
rules. In Russia they're making a whole new nation,

the people will rule. In America the people run the show, everyone has a chance. Even in England, things will change.

Did I see you?

MARGUERITE: So much hurt. You could not walk.

WILLIAM: Shrapnel in my leg. I can walk now. I saw you.

MARGUERITE: How were you safe?

WILLIAM: Albert and the Sergeant came to find me. But I saw you.

MARGUERITE: They are good friends. Your leg is hurt.

WILLIAM: Both.

MARGUERITE: I am careful.

WILLIAM: It's all right.

MARGUERITE: I don't touch.

Talk again.

WILLIAM: What shall I say?

MARGUERITE: Your family has big house.

WILLIAM: Oh no. We're not a great family.

MARGUERITE: You are alone.

WILLIAM: Yes. No. Not really. No. My wife.

MARGUERITE: Ah. You are good husband.

WILLIAM: We're fighting, they don't know. Your mates are dying in the mud and the stink and the blood.

MARGUERITE: And my brothers are killed.

WILLIAM: And we have to sort it out. They don't know, there's so much. It's far away. And your house is half shot to pieces.

MARGUERITE: My father is very tired.

WILLIAM: I will help.

MARGUERITE: You do help, William. You help me.

WILLIAM: I will help you, Marguerite.

MARGUERITE: I will look after your hurt.

WILLIAM: Marguerite. Your name is beautiful.

MARGUERITE: You are soft with me.

WILLIAM: You're like a lamb.

MARGUERITE: No William, I am a woman.

WILLIAM: You're a beautiful woman.

MARGUERITE: I pray this year fighting will not kill our crops. My brothers were good farmers. We had a big harvest, many beef, pigs.

WILLIAM: Marguerite, the world will be different. I feel it. People like us from all the nations will come together, people who work the land, work the factories, make the goods. Women will have the vote and help change the way we organise. Out of all of this filthy war we'll build a new world where freedom and fairness are stronger than land and money; where the people who do the work are the people who share in the rewards; where the colonies are decently governed and their people given all the benefits of a modern, democratic world. The Germans have no chance to fight back now. The Americans are here, huge numbers of them backing up our divisions. It's all going one way and this awful war will be won with the help of the great democratic country over the sea. They're all for one, we shall be all for one, everyone equal and free.

MARGUERITE: Let us lie in the sun.

WILLIAM: Do you vote?

MARGUERITE: The sun is in the leaves.

WILLIAM: There's no reason why women, everywhere, should not vote. Women are just as capable as men, they can go to classes to learn about politics, although many of them are very bright already about it. There was one woman who came to our branch –

MARGUERITE rises slowly to her knees and gently straddles WILLIAM

WILLIAM   Oh, Marguerite.

MARGUERITE bends to kiss WILLIAM. M. LEPINE comes

LEPINE: Mais qu'est-ce que tu fais ici?

MARGUERITE: Oh Papa!

LEPINE: Lève-toi. Tu m'a dis que tu allerait chercher du pain. Mister Randall, you stand up please. Marguerite, va t'en chez nous, immédiatement. Non, parle pas.

WILLIAM: Sir, you must forgive me.

LEPINE: Say nothing please, Mister Randall.

WILLIAM: Marguerite is not to blame.

LEPINE: You are right Mister Randall. You make the mistake.
            Marguerite, j'ai dit, va t'en chez nous. Allez. Mister
            Randall, follow me. We will speak to the officer.

MARGUERITE, WILLIAM, Lépine go

Scene Eleven

1941, the Randalls' kitchen
JOYCE (22) WILLIAM (55)
JOYCE is listening to the radio.

WILLIAM comes

WILLIAM: Where's your mother?

JOYCE: Out with Auntie Vera.

WILLIAM: I walked back. Great hole in the road down by the
hospital.

JOYCE: From last night?

WILLIAM: The maternity wing.

JOYCE: Oh, no, poor things.

WILLIAM: Babies in the rubble.

JOYCE: You couldn't see them.

WILLIAM: Someone sees them. Someone has to see dead children,
dead mothers. Who does this?

JOYCE: They don't care where they drop the bombs.

WILLIAM: We do it Joyce, we're just as bad.

JOYCE: No Dad, I'm sure our people are much more careful.
We try to hit / their factories and -

WILLIAM: We're just the same. Our boys, bombing at night, they
have no idea / where they're dropping -

JOYCE: They must do. It said in the paper how well they're
            trained.

WILLIAM: It's nonsense. They've no idea.

JOYCE: They do, Dad. John was saying / to me -

WILLIAM: What was John saying? Who's John?

JOYCE: I met him / the other day -

WILLIAM: Your mother gets very worried about all the boys you're
            off with.

JOYCE: She doesn't need to worry.

WILLIAM: Who's this John, then?

JOYCE: He's attached to the Air Ministry.

WILLIAM: And he thinks he knows all about night-flying, does he?
            Well, they're scrabbling through bricks looking for dead
            babies down the road. What does he think about that?

JOYCE: That's nothing to do with him. What's the matter, Dad?

WILLIAM: This is no place for you, Joyce, you and your Johns and
            Jims and whoever they are.

JOYCE: They're not Johns and Jims. I have friends and we're
            living and working through this war. Just like you and
            Mum and everyone else.

WILLIAM: Get away from it. I've seen what men do to each other.
            Broken bodies crushed into the mud, towns and
            villages smashed into the ground, old men running the
            show and Johns and Jims slicing open their stomachs
            with bayonets.

JOYCE: Dad stop it!

WILLIAM: I've seen it. Blood and stink and bones. And you'll get
              caught in it.

JOYCE: I'm in it, Dad, I'm in it.

WILLIAM: Everyone's forgotten. We sorted it out. We stopped the
              killing.

JOYCE: You stayed in Belgium to sort it out. You never talk
              about it.

WILLIAM:

              No more to say, Joyce. Long time ago.

JOYCE: Now we're doing it again.

WILLIAM: No more to say.

JOYCE: Tell me, Dad. It was important to you.

WILLIAM: We lost thousands of men all over that blasted place.
              Now we're losing babies down the road.

JOYCE: Why can't we stop it?

WILLIAM: We thought we did. We were putting it back together.
              We failed. It's too hard, there's too much money too
              many / people at the top -

JOYCE: What /money?

WILLIAM: - who don't want it to change.

JOYCE: You don't believe that. You're out every night, endless
              meetings to organize for change.

WILLIAM: Our men are dying again. We're up against the Germans again, France and Belgium are worse off than when all our mates were killed.

JOYCE: We can't give up. When you were young you did what you had to do. So will we. We'll go on fighting until it stops. John's working all hours, we all are.

WILLIAM: Who is this John?

JOYCE: Someone I met.

WILLIAM: Are you going to bring him home?

JOYCE: I don't know yet.

WILLIAM: Your mother worries about you.

JOYCE: There's nothing to worry about.

WILLIAM: You're out a lot.

JOYCE: So are you.

WILLIAM: That's different.

JOYCE: Mum's on her own.

WILLIAM: She's not, she's got all sorts of people she sees, people are in and out all the time. I hope you're taking care of yourself when you're out with these boys.

JOYCE: I'm always careful.

WILLIAM: There's many who aren't.

JOYCE: It's fun up in town – people want to have a good time. Everyone's coming and going.

WILLIAM: You find someone nice and stick to him.

JOYCE: I think John might be nice.

WILLIAM: Well, let's have a look at him.

JOYCE: Not yet. I'll get to know him a bit better.

WILLIAM: I want to meet him.

JOYCE: No.

WILLIAM: Do it Joyce. Your Mum wants to meet him and for you
to stay at home a bit more.

JOYCE: You stay at home. You're always out with those smelly
old men at the Union, all talk and tobacco.

WILLIAM: Now then.

JOYCE: Stay at home. Like you didn't do when I was born.
Like when Mum needed you to look after her and me.
Like when I was alive, not like these babies down the
road, you can't look after them / any more –

WILLIAM: Now Joyce / what –

JOYCE: Look after Mum. It's us young ones who are fighting.
I'm going up to town. Tell Mum I'll be all right. I'm
going to stay with John.

JOYCE goes

Scene Twelve

1943, the Randall's kitchen
BLANCHE (58), ALBERT (56), JOYCE (24), MARGERY (52)
BLANCHE and ALBERT are at the table

JOYCE and MARGERY come

JOYCE: I just got to the station in time.

MARGERY: Blanche dear, thank goodness –

ALBERT: Here you are!

JOYCE: Just in time.

MARGERY: What a time.

BLANCHE: I'll put the kettle on.

ALBERT: Where are your bags?

JOYCE: The station was crammed.

MARGERY: Blanche, don't get up. They're at the station.

JOYCE: I'll do it.

JOYCE goes

MARGERY: My, what a young lady she's turned into.

ALBERT: Looking lovelier all the time.

BLANCHE: Joyce is –

MARGERY: So grown up. You have done well, Blanche.

BLANCHE: She's very busy.

MARGERY: I see you in her.

ALBERT: She keeps the boys on their toes.

MARGERY: I've no doubt about that.

BLANCHE: That's enough, Albert.

MARGERY: She's straight out of a fashion magazine.

ALBERT: Takes after her mother.

MARGERY: I think she does, too.

BLANCHE: Get on with you, Albert.

ALBERT: I'll give Joyce a hand with the tray.

ALBERT goes

MARGERY: It's so good to see you. I haven't been back for so long.

BLANCHE: We've made up your bed.

MARGERY: It's like coming home.

BLANCHE: We've put you in the front. There's sometimes a draught, the window's a bit sideways. I've put a couple of extra blankets in the cupboard. What about your bags?

MARGERY: How's Will?

BLANCHE: Oh he's fine, same as ever.

MARGERY: Planning the revolution? The bags can wait.

BLANCHE: Digging the cellar slowed him down. After you were posted he built us a whole room under the house. Kept us safe. Took months.

JOYCE and ALBERT come with tea

ALBERT: Here we are.

MARGERY: Under the house?

ALBERT: When did you last have a proper cup of tea?

JOYCE: And cake.

MARGERY: What a homecoming!

JOYCE: How long can you stay?

MARGERY: I don't know – I may be sent for any minute – or not – but I'm not going to settle on you like an old duck.

ALBERT: You must come over to us – Vera won't let you go off again without coming over.

MARGERY: I'd love to. And I mustn't forget there's a small parcel for you Joyce in my bag.

ALBERT: Vera will be after me. Come over with Will and Blanche, we'll have a drink and you can tell us all your secrets.

BLANCHE: She can't do that Albert, don't be daft.

ALBERT: We'll winkle something out of her. I'm off. Lovely tea.

ALBERT goes

JOYCE: I wish you could tell us where you've been.

MARGERY: All over the place. Seen all sorts of strange sights.

JOYCE: Tell me. Everything's always the same here.

BLANCHE: People come through, we never know who's coming or going.

JOYCE: No but Aunt Margery has / been –

MARGERY: God, not 'aunt' any more, Joyce. You're far too grown up for that.

JOYCE: You've been to exotic places.

MARGERY: Hot as the desert, strange dens in bazaars, cold as ice with wolves in the forests.

JOYCE: Have you had mysterious affairs?

BLANCHE: Margery's only just sat down.

MARGERY: Dozens.

JOYCE: Tell, tell.

MARGERY: One day when all this is over. Perhaps. When you show me your secret room. Will dug out a whole room?

JOYCE: It's cosy if you don't worry about the mice.

BLANCHE: There aren't any mice / dear –

JOYCE: I've seen / one –

BLANCHE: We haven't had to use it in a while.

MARGERY: Let's hope never again.

BLANCHE: Joyce was up and down in the train all through the
            bombs and the fire. I was worried sick.

JOYCE: I got used to it, you just carry on. I'm going to change,
            I'm going out soon. I'll take the tray.

JOYCE goes

BLANCHE:

MARGERY: Well?

BLANCHE:

MARGERY: You asked me to / come –

BLANCHE: You must be tired.

MARGERY: I was exhausted but the tea's refreshing.

BLANCHE:

MARGERY: It's refreshing.

BLANCHE: Where would I go? Even if I wanted to. Which I don't.

MARGERY: Do you want to?

BLANCHE: No. Not now. I wouldn't think of it. There's a war on.

MARGERY: Not for ever?

BLANCHE: And Joyce.

MARGERY: What is she 23, 24?

BLANCHE: Yes.

MARGERY: And looking like she does. She'll have someone to look
           after her.

BLANCHE: Too many.

MARGERY: Never too many, not at her age.

BLANCHE: I worry. She keeps talking about this John, but she
           won't bring him home.

MARGERY: You asked me to come. How's Will?

BLANCHE: He doesn't tell me.

MARGERY: You must know.

BLANCHE: I've never known what he wants.

MARGERY: What does he come home to?

BLANCHE: His home. His daughter.

MARGERY: And you.

BLANCHE: He doesn't talk to me.

MARGERY: He never used to shut up.

BLANCHE: He might have talked to you. You made him laugh. In
           the old days. Your tea's getting cold. You and Albert,
           you could make him laugh. You laughed when you
           danced with him.

MARGERY: It's thirty years.

BLANCHE: Albert and you got me into this. I wouldn't be here –

MARGERY: Where would you / be?

BLANCHE: Safe at home.

MARGERY: You are at home. Will's made you safe, you and Joyce.

BLANCHE: They're safe. I'm on my own.

MARGERY: People are always here Blanche. I bump into them, in godforsaken places. People know you. You're good to them.

BLANCHE: He doesn't know me. He just expects me to be here.

MARGERY: You sleep with him.

BLANCHE:

MARGERY: Don't you?

BLANCHE: I've got used to it.

MARGERY: Well don't get used to it. If you're not happy change it. Do something about it.

BLANCHE: What can I do?

MARGERY: We're in the middle of a war. A bomb might drop at any minute. I've been / in places –

BLANCHE: You're telling me I don't understand, like him.

MARGERY: It's your life, Blanche. If it's wrong, change it.

BLANCHE: You made my bed. Why did you do that to me? Why didn't you marry him?

MARGERY: Don't tell me it's my fault. I'm not responsible. No-one is. Except you. Especially now.

BLANCHE: You've not drunk your tea.

MARGERY: Stop looking after people, Blanche. Look after yourself.
            Look after Will. Make him warm. Make him see you.

BLANCHE: Joyce –

MARGERY: Can look after herself.

JOYCE comes

MARGERY: Joyce, let's walk to the station. Remind me to look in
            my bag.

JOYCE: Goodnight, Mum.

Scene Thirteen

1944, the Randalls' kitchen
WILLIAM (58), BLANCHE (59), ALBERT (57), JOYCE (25), TED (60)
WILLIAM is at the table. BLANCHE and JOYCE listen to the radio
carrying war reports .

ALBERT and TED come

JOYCE: Uncle, you're late.

BLANCHE: Are you staying for tea?

TED: The trains are out, the main bridge at the junction is
            gone. I've got a lift coming to pick me up from here, if
            that's all right.

ALBERT: I thought you were on duty up in town.

JOYCE: I'm on tomorrow night.

ALBERT: Sleeping under the desks.

JOYCE: It's so uncomfortable.

ALBERT: Depends who you've got to keep you company.

JOYCE: Uncle!

BLANCHE: That's enough, Albert.

ALBERT: You've got to have some fun, Blanche. Joyce's a lovely
            young girl, you can't hide her in the cellar, war or no
            war.

TED: Bad influence, Albert Kerridge.

ALBERT: Me? Pure as the driven. Vera never lets me out of her
            sight long enough to get into trouble.

TED: You don't remember when I had you under guard?
            Chasing off across the fields after some mademoiselle.

JOYCE: You never told me about that, Uncle.

ALBERT: He's making it all up. No time for shilly-shallying.

WILLIAM: Too busy dodging the shells.

BLANCHE: Too busy to come home.

JOYCE: Maybe it's coming to an end. They say there's big troop
            movements / on the coast -

TED: Keep what you hear to yourself, Joyce.

JOYCE: We must invade, it's got to stop. We can't go on fighting
            each other every twenty years.

WILLIAM: It'll stop. When the war's over, there'll be an election.
            We'll form a proper Labour government, put Beveridge
            into action, nationalise the banks, the big industries.
            They'll bring back the League of Nations, and
            Labour will be a big part of the international socialist
            movement.

TED: You hope.

WILLIAM: We have to, Ted. Look at the Electricity Board. The
            works council pulls together, the workers and the
            managers. When the war's over, we'll link up again
            with comrades in other countries, grow a network too
            strong for capital to roll it over and break into pieces.

TED: You said that when we were putting back the bits of
            Belgium.

BLANCHE: I'll put the kettle on.

BLANCHE goes

JOYCE: Dad, it's us young people who are going to have to do
            it.

ALBERT: You've got better things to think about.

JOYCE: You fought for a reason. You were young.

ALBERT: That was all Ted's fault.

TED: And I got you out of it, too.

ALBERT: That bloody horse.

TED: We needed you, Will.

ALBERT: And your Dad still thinks he's going to put the world to
            rights.

BLANCHE comes

TED: I'm off now.

TED goes

JOYCE: You've known him so long.

WILLIAM: He's a good man. Saved me.

BLANCHE: Kept you in Belgium.

Sound of warning air-raid siren, continuously

JOYCE: Wailing Winnie's early.

WILLIAM: Down we go. There's room for you, Albert. I'll call Ted,
              they can't go off now.

BLANCHE: I'll go upstairs for an extra blanket.

WILLIAM: I'll get them. You get down into the cellar.

JOYCE: Quickly, Dad.

ALBERT: Come on Blanche, I'll give you a hand to make up the
              bunks.

Blanche and Albert go

WILLIAM: Go on Joyce, you go down. Carry the teapot, cups are
              down there. I'll call Ted back in.

*JOYCE goes one way, WILLIAM another. Siren continues. Explosion,
sound of glass breaking. ALBERT comes. WILLIAM comes, covered in
dust, limping, coughing.*

WILLIAM: I saw Ted.

ALBERT: Oh Lord, Will.

WILLIAM: He was getting into the car. They both caught it.

JOYCE: I'll get my kit. See what I can do.

JOYCE goes

WILLIAM: Joyce! Come back in.

Scene Fourteen

1919, Belgium, the Lépines' kitchen
WILLIAM (33), Marguerite (28)

MARGUERITE: Another letter has come from your wife. You must open. There will be a picture of your daughter.

WILLIAM: Not now. They're far away.

MARGUERITE: They think you are far.

WILLIAM: I've never seen her. I don't know her.

MARGUERITE: But you have feelings for her.

WILLIAM: Do I?

MARGUERITE: You are a father. I see you know. All little children should see her father.

WILLIAM: We have work to do. We have to lay new cable, quarter by quarter. First the industrial, then the domestic.

MARGUERITE: William, you know so many thing. Your head will carry you away. It will carry you away from me, back to your little girl. And to your wife.

WILLIAM: Life will pick up. People can get about, buy their food, start their trades again. I will send some money for my daughter. Marguerite, I want you with me. We young ones must come together. You know how hard you work, all of you, for all the families in the village. I'll be with you, we'll work together, there are big things happening in Russia, they've created new model of how to make the whole of society work. We'll travel, you and me, and see how each country will grow out of the ruins.

MARGUERITE: I think they killed a lot of people.

WILLIAM: The killing's over. We stopped it. We pushed the
            Germans back, us and the Americans, and your people
            and the French, we all fought together – a new order, a
            clean sheet.

MARGUERITE: I don't know how you mean with sheets. I listen to
            you always. Sometimes I think you will make the future
            all by yourself.

WILLIAM: Not by myself. With you.

MARGUERITE: William, I cannot go away. I have to stay with my
            father. He needs me. My brothers are all gone.

WILLIAM: In the early morning, when you're still asleep, I look
            at each tiny hair on your golden arms and want to
            stroke every one. And when I hold you and you take
            me then I am at home, at peace, and from there we can
            ride together, ride and ride across all the world and we
            ride up to the tops of the highest mountains and see
            everything, everything, everything. And there is no
            more war.
                Don't cry, Marguerite, don't cry. Why are you
            crying?

Scene Fifteen

August 1945, the Randalls' kitchen
WILLIAM (59), BLANCHE (60), ALBERT (58), JOYCE (26)

BLANCHE: Has he actually said he's going to marry you?

JOYCE: He'd like to.

BLANCHE: Everything's so up in the air now.

JOYCE: It's over, Mum. At last, at last, at last we can start again, it's going to be so different. We won the war, we won the election. I think I'm in love with John.

BLANCHE: You've only once brought him home.

JOYCE: He's away at the moment. I'm waiting for a letter today.

BLANCHE: He's away quite a lot.

JOYCE: He's in the Ministry of Reconstruction. He'll probably have to go and look at what's needed in France and Belgium. Even Germany.

BLANCHE: Where is he now?

JOYCE: I'm waiting for a letter. Probably today.

BLANCHE: If he wants to marry you, where's he going to set up house?

JOYCE: It doesn't matter, we could go anywhere where he has to work. Or where I can work. I'm not just going to follow him around.

BLANCHE: Well, is he going to follow you around? I don't think so.

JOYCE: He loves me, Mum. We're going to work out a new life, we're putting ourselves at the service of the new society. It's so exciting.

BLANCHE: It may be, dear, but is he going to look after you?

JOYCE: I don't need looking after. I'm a grown woman.

BLANCHE: A proper husband should look after his wife.

JOYCE: John and I may get married, we may not.

BLANCHE: You said he wants to marry you.

JOYCE: You know what men say.

BLANCHE: You don't want to throw yourself away.

JOYCE: I'm not throwing myself anywhere. Any man I marry will be an equal partner. And I may not marry John. We may choose to be a couple and remain completely independent.

BLANCHE: Oh no dear, that wouldn't be right. What would people think?

JOYCE: We have a new world, new ways of living. I don't have to ask John what we're going to do.

BLANCHE: It was very different in my day.

JOYCE: Was it? Dad proposed to you.

BLANCHE: Then he went off to war.

JOYCE: But you married and he came back.

BLANCHE: Eventually. And I had you to look after.

JOYCE: I don't need looking after any more.

BLANCHE: Well what about a family? You're 26 after all. You don't
            want to find yourself stuck like I was.

JOYCE: That was me.

BLANCHE: I was all on my own, it was very hard. I'm just saying,
            you want to make sure this John is going to look after
            you when you have a baby.

JOYCE: We're not thinking about having a baby.

BLANCHE: I don't like it, dear. You've been out with lots of young
            men, sometimes you haven't come home when we've
            expected you and it was so dangerous, thank goodness,
            that's all stopped. But look at the mess everywhere, it'll
            take years to put right. You don't want to go rushing
            into marrying, not someone we've hardly met.

JOYCE: I'm not marrying him, I said – he's saying he wants to
            marry me.

BLANCHE: Did he say that?

Scene Sixteen

1920 Belgium, the Lépines' kitchen
WILLIAM (34), MARGUERITE (29), M. LEPINE (52)
WILLIAM, MARGUERITE and M. LEPINE at the kitchen table. M.
LEPINE reading the newspaper.

WILLIAM: Some of the units are staying on. Maybe six months.

MARGUERITE: Six months in the summer time.

M. LEPINE: C'est pas les vacances, l'été. Il y a beaucoup de choses à faire.

MARGUERITE: Oh Papa. William works very hard for us.

M. LEPINE: Sais pas, moi.

MARGUERITE: Papa, you are too bad. William, come.

MARGUERITE and WILLIAM move out of the kitchen

WILLIAM: I will ask them tomorrow. They could give us another wonderful summer.

MARGUERITE: William, I must say something.

WILLIAM: I love the sound of your voice.

MARGUERITE: You will not love it.

WILLIAM: I will always love it.

MARGUERITE: William, stop. Stop. You must go home William. Your daughter. She needs her father. I see in your eyes when your wife sends you pictures. Your daughter is growing into a little girl already. We have stolen some time from this war. You have been good to me, to my father. You have helped us to build our home again. Now you must go home and use your gifts. Give them to your daughter. Give them to your wife.

WILLIAM: Marguerite.

MARGUERITE: Shhh.

WILLIAM: Marguerite, I don't know them.

MARGUERITE: Shhh. You will.

WILLIAM: I don't know.

MARGUERITE: Your family needs you. Your little girl needs her father.

WILLIAM: I think about her.

MARGUERITE: I know.

WILLIAM: I think about how she will go to school. What she will learn.

MARGUERITE: I learn from my father.

WILLIAM: If I meet her. If she will forgive me.

MARGUERITE: There is nothing to forgive. You have done your duty.

They kiss. M. LEPINE comes

M. LEPINE: Monsieur. Mr Randall. I am losing my sons in war. Marguerite t'aime, je vois. I say merci, for the help you have made us. I know you have wife and child. Je ne dis rien de tous cela. But as I have a daughter, I know and Marguerite know that small child waits for you. You will be our friend. Au revoir.

LEPINE goes

MARGUERITE: I will never forget, you, dear William.

WILLIAM: I cannot leave. I love you.

MARGUERITE: I love you, William. And because I love you, I see in your eyes some pain.

WILLIAM: How can I go home?

MARGUERITE: Because where is your daughter and wife is your home. They are waiting for you. William. This is the way. For many nights I think about it. I speak to my father. This is the way. You are a father. Your child wishes to speak to you. And to hear you.

WILLIAM: I love you.

MARGUERITE: I will write you, tell you our news. I will help you pack your clothes.

MARGUERITE and WILLIAM go

Scene Seventeen

1946 , the Randalls' kitchen.
MARGERY (55), JOYCE (27), BLANCHE (61)
JOYCE and John's wedding party going on offstage

MARGERY: You reeled him in, then.

JOYCE: He's flopping about in my net.

MARGERY: I'm not surprised. You're looking gorgeous.

JOYCE: Don't be silly. I found some stuff last week and threw it together. Mum's friend at the draper's had it in the back somewhere.

MARGERY: He looks a very nice young man.

JOYCE: Not so young. He's actually 40.

MARGERY: Really? I wouldn't have / thought -

JOYCE: Don't tell Mum, please.

MARGERY: She doesn't know?

JOYCE: It's a bit difficult.

MARGERY: Your Mum and Dad've been very welcoming today.

JOYCE: They don't really like him.

MARGERY: You haven't given them much chance.

JOYCE: He got posted a lot. Like you. A lot of overseas postings. I haven't been anywhere.

MARGERY: You'll get the chance. You and John – if he's been about,
            he'll take you all over the place.

JOYCE: I can't wait. I just want to set off with him, just the two
            of us. Some far away hotel, cheap and clean, breeze in
            the window, a bed that doesn't squeak. I'm getting a bit
            carried away.

MARGERY: Your John will carry you away. Looks as if he's good in
            bed.

JOYCE: It can be a bit of a wrestling match. Sometimes it's
            rather sudden. I've ended up on his sitting room floor
            more than once.

MARGERY: On top or underneath?

JOYCE: I can't always tell.

MARGERY: Make sure it's half and half. Nice place?

JOYCE: He's moved out of his home. He's been married before.
            I daren't tell Mum and Dad. They'd be so upset.

MARGERY: Oh Joyce, you have dived in haven't you?

JOYCE: I can't help it, I don't regret anything, he wasn't happy
            and he makes me feel so free. I just want to wrap myself
            around him.

BLANCHE comes

MARGERY: I'm sure that suits him very well.

BLANCHE: They're cheerful in there.

MARGERY: I was telling Joyce how lovely she looks.

JOYCE: The dress is all down to Mum.

BLANCHE: It's nice material. The draper's girl let us have it quite cheap.

JOYCE: Her wedding present.

BLANCHE: I did work for her mother years ago. They've always been good people.

MARGERY: It's come out beautifully. What have you got for going away?

JOYCE: I couldn't afford a whole outfit.

MARGERY: Your fine new husband won't mind.

BLANCHE: Some of his friends look very sharp.

JOYCE: Just a mix, new skirt and my best jacket.

MARGERY: Something frilly underneath.

JOYCE: One or two things.

MARGERY: I remember you and Will setting off, Blanche. That was a lovely wedding too.

BLANCHE: I've come in to find something more to give them. I didn't expect so many.

MARGERY: Never mind, you've provided plenty.

BLANCHE: Your John's got an appetite. Some of his women friends are so thin they can't have eaten for months.

JOYCE: They're all right Mum don't worry.

BLANCHE: I don't know what to say to them. They were looking round our rooms as though we were foreign. Do you know them?

JOYCE: One or two. I've met them, out with John.

BLANCHE: They're not like us.

MARGERY: New people are fun.

BLANCHE: One of them said something.

MARGERY: Different people are so interesting. The war has thrown us all together.

BLANCHE: She said you're much prettier than his first wife.

JOYCE:

BLANCHE: Why, Joyce?

JOYCE: I didn't / want to –

BLANCHE: Why are you doing this to us? Your father/ and I –

JOYCE: I'm not doing –

BLANCHE: You never bring him home –

JOYCE: I did –

BLANCHE: We went along with it, now we have these smart strangers in our house laughing at us. What have we done?

JOYCE: They'll go. I'll tell them to go.

MARGERY: You stay here, I'll tell them.

BLANCHE: You knew about this didn't you? I expect Will knows.

JOYCE: No he doesn't Mum I'm sorry/ I didn't want –

BLANCHE: I tried to look after you, bring you up clean and healthy and safe all through this horrible war. Now you run off with a married man.

JOYCE: He's not married he's married to me.

MARGERY: It's all right Joyce.

BLANCHE: No it's not all right. It's wicked. I've produced a wicked daughter who's driven me mad with worry, doesn't love me, doesn't care what I think.

MARGERY: Of course she does.

BLANCHE: And who are you to talk?

MARGERY: Who are you to make such a fuss? Joyce has won her freedom.

BLANCHE: Free as anything to go off and do what she likes. Mess up someone's marriage, laugh and dance all night with this sharp man we don't know. What happens when he gets tired of her?

JOYCE: He won't he won't. I'll make him happy.

BLANCHE: That's what you think.

MARGERY: Of course she will.

BLANCHE: That's what I thought. You'll be alone, and old.

MARGERY: Sit down, I'll make some tea.

ALBERT comes

ALBERT: Come on Joyce, we're all waiting. What a party! Your
            husband's got a glass in his hand. Time to cut the cake.

Scene Eighteen

May 1915, the English south coast
WILLIAM (29), BLANCHE (30)

BLANCHE: I've only once been to the sea. It's lovely, William. It's such a change.

WILLIAM: We came here when I was a boy. Come on up the cliff path, we'll see for miles on a day like this.

BLANCHE: Do you feel changed now we're married?

WILLIAM: Of course I do. This way. It's a bit steep at first.

BLANCHE: I don't mind. I'll follow you. I think I feel a bit light-headed.

WILLIAM: Sun and wind.

BLANCHE: No, being married. It takes a lot of getting used to.

WILLIAM: You're a lovely wife.

BLANCHE: Am I, William? I was worried at first.

WILLIAM: What about?

BLANCHE: I didn't know about it, what to do.

WILLIAM: You're doing fine, Blanche. You mustn't worry.

BLANCHE: Well, I'm not going to. There's no time for it. Look at the sea, it's so bright.

WILLIAM: And there, far away, you can just see France.

BLANCHE: I never believed you could.

WILLIAM: Just faintly. Come here, look, over there, just what looks like a low cloud, there. That's a cliff. Coast of France.

BLANCHE:

WILLIAM:

BLANCHE: It's quiet.

WILLIAM: They're stuck.

BLANCHE: And we're here in the sunshine.

WILLIAM: Sunny there. It makes me sick. Our people threw it away.

BLANCHE: I don't see how we could have stopped it, we couldn't do any more. We have to build it up again. Do you know what we should do, William? We should join forces. Your people at the Union of Democratic Control and my group at the ELFS. Wouldn't that be fine? We'll make a bigger noise against the war together. We're both getting new members each month. We'll march again. Let's do it together.

WILLIAM: I don't know Blanche.

BLANCHE: Come on William, it's up to us.

WILLIAM: I know it is, but / we can't…

BLANCHE: But what, but nothing. Think of them over there.

WILLIAM: They're stuck, like stupid wrestlers. Can't let go.

BLANCHE: That's why we have to make a bigger noise. You said it, you told me before the war. I learnt so much from you, William. I still do.

WILLIAM: That was then. We let it go. We had the power in our hands, the workers, the Trade Unions, here, Germany, France, Italy, we met each other, knew each other, saw the bosses for what they were.

BLANCHE: We still do.

WILLIAM: They caved in, all of them. All the socialist parties, they just fell into line. Lined up with the kings and the kaisers, to protect the fatherlands. Now they're lined up marching towards the guns. Over there. We can hear them.

BLANCHE: No we can't, not now. Don't let's spoil the day. Let's walk on, William. Give me your arm.

WILLIAM:

BLANCHE: Don't be sad.

WILLIAM:

BLANCHE: I was talking to Margery. She's lucky, she just inherited a little bit of money from her aunt. She's going to put it by towards a house. She spoke to her landlord. That's an interesting idea, isn't it?

WILLIAM:

BLANCHE: I'd like to think about it for us, William.

WILLIAM: We haven't the money to buy our house.

BLANCHE: Not now, but we could save. You'll go up a grade soon
and I've got so much sewing work. I'll tell you a secret,
shall I?

WILLIAM: What's that?

BLANCHE: I'll not tell.

WILLIAM: Tell me.

BLANCHE: You must tease it out of me.

WILLIAM: Must I?

BLANCHE: I'll not tell.

WILLIAM: I'll have to tickle you.

BLANCHE: No I won't.

WILLIAM: Come here, come here.

BLANCHE: No you can't catch me.

WILLIAM: I've got you.

BLANCHE: No I won't.

WILLIAM: I'll tickle. I'm tickling.

BLANCHE: No, no stop.

WILLIAM: I'm tickling.

BLANCHE: I'll tell. I'll tell.

WILLIAM: Tell me.

BLANCHE: I've put some money by.

WILLIAM: How much?

BLANCHE: From the sewing. You know I borrowed the new Singer. It's so fast. I'm doing twice as much.

WILLIAM: You're so good at it.

BLANCHE: And with your good job, we'll be able to save some more. One day, we could think about buying our house.

WILLIAM: It's a long road.

BLANCHE: One day.

WILLIAM: One day maybe. After the war.

BLANCHE: Yes. So we must raise our voices to stop it.

WILLIAM: Our voices won't stop it.

BLANCHE: Yes they will, we'll join forces, the women and the men.

WILLIAM: They've set a machine rolling that can't hear our voices.

BLANCHE: We'll break the machine.

WILLIAM: Over there. Two giant machines shoving against each other. The big industries want it to go on. Every shell that explodes makes them more money.

BLANCHE: I know that, you told me, you make all your speeches.

WILLIAM: And our people fell apart. Your Pankhursts joined the war effort without blinking. So much for / votes for women.

BLANCHE: Not Sylvia. And not your people.

WILLIAM: Our people are split. Albert may be right.

BLANCHE: Oh no.

WILLIAM: Only one way to end it.

BLANCHE: No William.

WILLIAM: Push back the other machine.

BLANCHE: You don't believe that. You know you don't.

WILLIAM: What else?

BLANCHE: I don't believe it either. You and I agree, William.

WILLIAM: We do – the kings, the kaisers, the bosses, the governments – they all want the biggest machines. We have to break the machines. But most of our people signed up for war, Blanche.

BLANCHE: I didn't. You didn't. I don't want to talk about it. Let's go home. The sun's going in.

WILLIAM: We have to push them back.

BLANCHE: I'm going down. Come on William, let's go back to the station.

WILLIAM:

BLANCHE: I'm going down to the station.

Dear Julian,

Break a leg!

With love,

8 March 2018

Scene Nineteen

1966, the Randalls' kitchen
WILLIAM (80), BLANCHE (81), JOYCE (47), ALBERT (79).
The television is on, broadcasting late evening news on the night of the
General Election[7].

BLANCHE: That George Brown is a disgrace – he drinks.

ALBERT: The whole lot of 'em are shifty, if you ask me. Where are the working people in that crowd?

BLANCHE: I like Barbara Castle, she makes sense. She won't be pushed around.

ALBERT: True Labour people don't get much of a look-in – Ray Gunter, Jim Griffiths – mind you, they're Welsh.

BLANCHE: Wilson's out of touch.

JOYCE comes

ALBERT: How does it look?

JOYCE: The office is packed. They're all going off to the count. I'll go back a bit later.

BLANCHE: You've had no sleep for days.

JOYCE: We'll have a clear majority tomorrow morning.

BLANCHE: John telephoned. Said he hadn't seen you.

WILLIAM: I didn't fight the Germans, run the power, fight another war to have George Brown running the show.

JOYCE: You don't want the Tories in. He knows where I am.

BLANCHE: He said good luck.

WILLIAM: I was down the Electricity / Board.

JOYCE: We've made our own luck / this time.

WILLIAM: They were talking about cutting staff numbers and I said 'Half a mo, we're serving the people, not running a business for shareholders.'

BLANCHE: He was being nice.

ALBERT: Did they put you back in your box?

WILLIAM: They think I'm a silly old fool.

BLANCHE: He sounded a bit far away.

JOYCE: John's only at home. They still love you down there, Dad.

BLANCHE: You'd think so, the amount of time he spends.

ALBERT: Better than mouldering away at home.

BLANCHE: Where can I go? Is he going away again?

JOYCE: I don't know. You'd better come and stay with us, for a bit.

BLANCHE: No, dear, you're always having us. You've got your own life.

JOYCE: We haven't talked about it.

WILLIAM: Look at Germany, they've got works councils, workers represented all the way up / the business –

JOYCE: I must get back to / the office.

WILLIAM: – because after the war, we sorted it all out for them.

JOYCE: We all worked together. All for one.

ALBERT: We didn't get invaded was the main thing.

BLANCHE: It's all over now. You can't do any more.

JOYCE: I have to. We had to grow up very fast, when we were
            young, There's so much to do. He's got to see that I 'm
            alive.

ALBERT: We came out of it with a cracking Labour government
            then.

WILLIAM: Not like this lot.

JOYCE: It's not over till we know the result.

WILLIAM: All over the place.

BLANCHE: He said on the phone the polls say we're going to win.

WILLIAM: You need a head of steam, keep the Tories at bay, and
            drive on with re-distribution and / public services.

BLANCHE: He sounded / far away.

WILLIAM: No shilly-shallying, join the Common Market, build on
            what the Germans and the French have done.

JOYCE: That's what we're doing, Dad, we're in government.
            We've held on.

BLANCHE: Isn't he at your house?

WILLIAM: You've worked hard at it, I'll say that.

JOYCE: I suppose so.

BLANCHE: You're tired out, dear.

JOYCE: Stop fussing. I'm going back for the count.

BLANCHE: I'll make up a bed for you here.

JOYCE: No, Mum, I've got to go back.

BLANCHE: It's all over now, surely.

JOYCE: There's a lot to do while the count's going on, then I'll
            go home.

ALBERT: Here they come.

JOYCE: I've got to go.

BLANCHE: I'll make you some breakfast in the morning.

JOYCE: It's all right, Mum. We've done it, I'm sure of it. The
            television reports early poll results .

BLANCHE: Telephone John, dear, if you can.

TV sound fades

Scene Twenty

1967, the Randalls' bedroom
JOYCE (48), WILLIAM (81), ALBERT (80).
WILLIAM is in bed, half-asleep.

JOYCE: I don't know whether he'll understand.

ALBERT: He's your Dad, and he's always loved you.

JOYCE: That's why it's hard.

            Dad. Are you awake? I didn't want to wake you up. Are
            you all right?

WILLIAM: How are you?

JOYCE: I'm all right, Dad. You're looking much better than last
            week.

ALBERT: Right as rain, Will.

WILLIAM: All right. Is Mum making some tea?

JOYCE: She's out.

WILLIAM: She'll be back.

JOYCE: Dad. I need to tell you something.

WILLIAM: I wouldn't mind some tea.

ALBERT: On my way. Stand by your beds.

ALBERT goes

JOYCE: Dad, it's about John and me.

WILLIAM: John?

JOYCE: You know, John. I live with him. Lived.

WILLIAM: John. Yes.

JOYCE: We've decided we're not going to be together any more.

WILLIAM: He gets about.

JOYCE: Yes he does, but when he comes back, we're not going to be together.

WILLIAM: Oh yes?

JOYCE: He's gone off with somebody else. He's decided he wants to be with someone younger and I suppose he thinks prettier. She's got a child.

WILLIAM: Is he going to look after her child?

JOYCE: He's ripped us apart. She's taken him away from me.

WILLIAM: How old's the child?

JOYCE: I don't know. A girl.

WILLIAM:

JOYCE: Dad / –

WILLIAM: Have you told Mum?

JOYCE: Not yet.

WILLIAM: I expect she knows.

JOYCE: She didn't like him.

WILLIAM: She was worried about you.

JOYCE: She shouldn't have been.

            Perhaps she should.

WILLIAM: How old's the girl?

JOYCE: I don't know, Dad. I haven't asked I don't care how old
            the girl is.

ALBERT comes

JOYCE: I didn't want children. We talked, we travelled, we
            organized.

WILLIAM: I used to make things for you. Could've done for a little
            grandson or daughter.

ALBERT: Here's your tea.

JOYCE: Dad, I'm sorry.

WILLIAM: Never mind about that. Thanks, Albert.

JOYCE: It's too late. I can't start again.

ALBERT: Of course you can.

WILLIAM: You did good work back then.

JOYCE: What for?

WILLIAM: You had to do it all over again. People forget.

ALBERT: Vera said you'll be out finding someone new in no
            time.

JOYCE: Did you forget me?

WILLIAM: No.

ALBERT: It's hard now, but you're young, it'll pass. You've got plenty of friends – someone'll turn up, you'll see.

WILLIAM: I came back for you.

JOYCE: John won't come back.

WILLIAM: Your Mum was right.

JOYCE: I don't want him back. He's broken us.

WILLIAM: She was very strong.

ALBERT: Something will turn up.

JOYCE: No it won't, I haven't got the spark for it. I can't fly any more.

ALBERT: Blanche is back.

JOYCE: She won't be surprised.

WILLIAM: I came back.

JOYCE: I've so much to do. The government's in a mess, they're starting to fight each other, the pound's dropping all the time. They think Wilson will devalue.

WILLIAM: I came back for you. I didn't / know you.

JOYCE: The balance of payments is getting worse every month. I need to organize the meeting. People are never there.

ALBERT: I'll tell Blanche you're here.

WILLIAM: Has John gone off with another woman?

JOYCE: I just told you.

WILLIAM: Got a daughter.

JOYCE: I must go back to the office.

WILLIAM: Is he going to look after her?

JOYCE: I don't know, Dad. And I really don't care. He's torn
            us up, I don't know what I'm going to do. I work and
            work and work looking after him, keep our house nice,
            put up with it all the times he was away, smile when he
            comes back get on with it when he's here join in with
            his plans and friends and then he just rips it up fancies
            someone with fresher tits and leaves me mothering
            the Labour party. Is this my life? Is this what you had
            me for? I'm in a mess, the government's in a mess, the
            country's in a mess. Mum's come back with more ham
            and lettuce and my own house is full of a lifetime's
            rubbish. Is this what you came back for?

Scene Twenty-One

Summer 1968, the Randall's kitchen
JOYCE (49), BLANCHE (83)

BLANCHE: I did get used to him.

JOYCE: Well, he's gone.

BLANCHE: I'm sorry for you dear.

JOYCE: Thank you Mum. It doesn't matter.

BLANCHE:

JOYCE:

BLANCHE: Will you make some tea?

JOYCE: Do you want tea?

BLANCHE: I thought you might like some.

JOYCE: You were right about him.

BLANCHE: You had your work. Dad's always talking about his daughter 'holding the Labour Party together'.

JOYCE: He can't remember much of that now.

BLANCHE: It comes back. He's got a bit worse lately.

JOYCE: You need to get some help in.

BLANCHE: I can manage.

JOYCE: You can't, Mum, it's very tiring for you. It's not going to get better.

BLANCHE: Come and read to him again. He likes it. It settles him down.

JOYCE: I'll try. I'm very busy.

BLANCHE: I know you're always busy dear.

JOYCE: I've been offered a new job.

BLANCHE: Have you? That's very nice. Are you going to run the National Executive Committee?

JOYCE: I'm leaving the Labour Party.

BLANCHE: How can you leave the Labour Party?

JOYCE: I'm leaving England. I'm going to work in Brussels. On our application to join the Common Market. They've asked me to research how it will be when workers are moving freely between all the countries.

BLANCHE: When will we see you? What about your father?

JOYCE: That's why you need to get some help in. I'm not going to be here.

BLANCHE: I can't do it on my own.

JOYCE: That's what I'm telling you.

            Soon. Next week.

BLANCHE: What about me?

JOYCE: I'll come back and see you. I've been in touch with the
             Social Services.

BLANCHE: We don't need that sort of help. They come and go. You
             never know who they are.

JOYCE: They can be very nice.

BLANCHE: You're our family.

JOYCE: I'll still be your family. Working in Brussels.

BLANCHE: You're very hard, Joyce.

             You were always hard. Right from the beginning. You
             were hard when you were born. Hard when I was
             on my own. Hard when your father came back. He
             thought the world of you, had no time for me.

JOYCE: Now that's not true, Mum. Don't upset yourself.

BLANCHE: You go off, you make sure you're all right. We'll
             manage.

JOYCE: It's a wonderful opportunity, Mum. Working for our
             future.

BLANCHE: Your father had his head in the clouds, socialist this,
             socialist that, international socialists.

JOYCE: He believed in it. He tried his best.

BLANCHE: I had to drag him back from trying his best with
             another woman.

JOYCE:

BLANCHE:

JOYCE: You've lived a long life since then. You're the heart and
              soul of this house – people coming and going, so much
              in the war, you gave everyone a home. You brought me
              up, you looked after me. Forgive him for that.

BLANCHE:

JOYCE: I'll make some tea.

BLANCHE: I don't want your tea. Go off to Brussels. Go off to
              your government jobs. I met the government, you
              forget that. I was fighting for the vote, sixty years
              ago, so women could vote here in England not run
              off somewhere else. I looked after my mother when
              I was fighting for the vote, waiting for your father to
              come back, not knowing whether he was dead or alive,
              looking after you when I didn't know what to do. Now
              you're all right, fancy free, no husband, no children,
              dancing around. Somewhere over in Europe.

JOYCE: I'll put the kettle on.

Scene Twenty-Two

Summer 1971. A hospital bed
WILLIAM (84), NURSE (30)
WILLIAM is in bed, breathing with difficulty.

NURSE: Your daughter will be back tomorrow. You haven't had much of your soup.

WILLIAM: It's awful. Are we still in France?

NURSE: No, dear, this is England.

WILLIAM: Did Albert catch it?

NURSE: Who's Albert, dear?

WILLIAM: Albert.

Are you here? Joyce is coming now. We're going back to Blighty.

NURSE: She'll be here soon.

WILLIAM: Is Joyce coming?

NURSE: She's coming soon.

WILLIAM: Joyce is coming soon. Through the blitz and fires. I kept her safe. You there, Albert? We're going back. Is Joyce coming? I need to see her before I go back. Pretty little girl. Pretty like you. Are you here? We could live here. None of that in our war. Tanks driving all over the battlefield, chopping up the wires.

He coughs and has difficulty breathing

WILLIAM: Albert was behind me. I shinned up the wall.

He holds the NURSE's hand more tightly

WILLIAM: Is Joyce coming? I could help in your father's farm.

NURSE: She'll be here soon, dear.

WILLIAM: What's your name?

NURSE: Margery.

WILLIAM: I don't know any Margery. I'm stuck here I have to get back. Marguerite. Help me pack my case and we'll go. Marguerite. We'll soon finish it. Let's walk out and pick some flowers. Your father will chase me. Joyce will pick the flowers with us.

NURSE: That would be nice, dear.

WILLIAM: Not you. Blanche is a good woman. Joyce? I have to get back. Pack my bag.

See that bird?

Did you have a baby?

NURSE: Yes, a little girl. Grown up now.

WILLIAM:

NURSE: Shall I take your soup?

WILLIAM: See that bird?

NURSE: I'll take it, you've had a bit.

WILLIAM: Did you have a baby?

NURSE: Yes, a little girl.

WILLIAM: Was she mine?

NURSE: Let's plump up these pillows.

NURSE goes. WILLIAM sinks onto pillows.

WILLIAM: I'll get back just need to pack Joyce'll be here.

            Albert! Look at that bird. Watch out!

WILLIAM catches his breath. Coughs. His throat rattles. Faint noise of hammering

WILLIAM: Joyce!

Hammering

WILLIAM: Joyce.

WILLIAM dies. NURSE comes, closes his eyes.

Noise of hammering steadily increases

Scene Twenty-Three

1922, the Randalls' kitchen
WILLIAM (36), ALBERT (35), BLANCHE (37)

BLANCHE: You should stop now.

WILLIAM: *(offstage)* We haven't finished the window-frame.

BLANCHE: Joyce is asleep.

ALBERT comes. Hammering continues

BLANCHE: There's another letter from Belgium.

ALBERT: Letter?

BLANCHE: You know as well as he does.

WILLIAM comes

BLANCHE Another one.

WILLIAM: You'd better give it to me.

ALBERT: We're all here now.

BLANCHE: And this is where he's staying.

WILLIAM: Let me have the letter, please.

BLANCHE: No, William.

WILLIAM: Blanche, as your husband.

BLANCHE: My husband. What sort of a husband are you? That child is nearly three. I looked after her on my own for two years.

ALBERT: Vera's been helping, Blanche.

BLANCHE: That girl follows you around as soon as you come home from work. She worships the ground you walk on. But what about me? Where were you when she was born? How was I supposed to live?

WILLIAM: You know we had work to do.

BLANCHE: I know what work you were doing. Don't think I don't know. I looked after you when you came home wounded.

ALBERT: He was bad, Blanche.

BLANCHE: Not bad enough, evidently. You stayed, Albert. Vera made sure of that. But not him. As soon as he could walk, he was off again. You were needed at the front, you said. Ted Turner couldn't do without you. I believed you.

ALBERT: Will's trade was important.

BLANCHE: More important than me, evidently. I don't know why you bothered to marry me in the first place. You were thrilled when you signed up. I didn't know what to think. Why has he married me when he wants to get away?

WILLIAM: We had to do our duty.

BLANCHE: Most of them came home to their wives and children after they'd done their duty. Not you. You stayed away.

WILLIAM: I had more to do.

BLANCHE: Oh yes, a lot more. I know why you didn't come home.
             You had that woman.

ALBERT: Now, Blanche.

BLANCHE: You get out, Albert. He's had enough good works from
             you.

WILLIAM: You'd better go, Albert. I'll see you tomorrow.

ALBERT goes

WILLIAM: Blanche, listen to me.

BLANCHE: Listen to you? You've nothing to say to me. I looked
             after our child for two years before you came home.
             Now you're here, she's all over you. She's very hard to
             me, she doesn't love me.

WILLIAM: Of course she does, Blanche. You look after her, she's
             growing up.

BLANCHE: You don't love me. You don't want me. I've had no
             married life with you, that you promised.

WILLIAM: I'm here.

BLANCHE: You're writing to her, that woman. I see you looking
             out of the window. I see you playing with Joyce. I never
             see you looking at me. I don't know why you're here. I
             don't know why I'm here.

WILLIAM: Of course you know why you're here. We're married.
             We have a life to live.

BLANCHE: You don't know what you're saying.

WILLIAM: Now that I'm back, now that we have our daughter.
            We're together again, Blanche, just like before. We'll
            carry on the work we were doing. Together again, dear.

BLANCHE: I hated this war, but it gripped you. You listened for the
            guns, you said you could hear them in France when
            you stood up on the hill. One day in a flash you waved
            your shilling at me, you were gone. You wrote to me a
            few times. You didn't say much. Only that when it was
            all over the world would be a better place. Maybe for
            you. And when you came back, scarcely able to walk,
            raw wounds in your legs, I looked after you. I bathed
            you and changed your bandages. And you were rough
            with me and I felt it in my stomach.

WILLIAM: I had to go back.

BLANCHE: You wanted to go back to her. You wanted to make
            your brave new world after the war with somebody
            else, not with your wife, not with your child, not with
            me. That's what your grand war has done to you.

WILLIAM: Give me the letter, Blanche.

BLANCHE: You must stop writing to her.

WILLIAM: Give me the letter from her.

BLANCHE takes the letter from a pocket and tears it to small pieces

BLANCHE: That is the end of it William.
            I've done it.
            Now we have to live our lives.

WILLIAM moves close to BLANCHE and takes her elbow.

BLANCHE   Don't touch me.

Envoi

Silence, summer light

MARGUERITE, very pregnant, picks the petals from a flower. Sings

MARGUERITE: Après la guerre finie,
les soldats anglais partient.
Les mademoiselles toujours beaucoup pleuraient
Après la guerre finie.

End

Notes

1. http://www.la-croix.com/Culture/Musique/1914-1918-les-chansons-d-une-Grande-Guerre-2013-11-11-1059018, from 0:58 to 1:12 – this recording has the proper tune and words of La Madelon – to which the text of the troops' version was added.

2. https://www.youtube.com/watch?v=vtwYVvtOIuM, beginning to 1.14.

3. http://spartacus-educational.com/Wbillinghurst.htm

4. http://www.greatwar.co.uk/battles/second-ypres-1915/index.htm

5. http://www.bbc.co.uk/history/worldwars/wwone/mirror02_01.shtml

6. These two sentences are a quotation from: Kernahan, Coulson, *Experiences of a Recruiting Officer* (London: Hodder and Stoughton, 1915).

7. https://www.youtube.com/watch?v=9HbBG2sZeeA, 12:00 to 12:40.